HELICOPTER PILOT

PILOT

(**MICHAEL COX**)

**Illustrated by
Stuart Holmes**

SCHOLASTIC

Scholastic Children's Books
Commonwealth House, 1–19 New Oxford Street,
London, WC1A 1NU, UK
A division of Scholastic Ltd
London ~ New York ~ Toronto ~ Sydney ~ Auckland
Mexico City ~ New Delhi ~ Hong Kong

Published in the UK by Scholastic Ltd, 2004

Text copyright © Michael Cox, 2004
Illustrations copyright © Stuart Holmes, 2004
ISBN 0 439 97742 8

Contents

Introduction

Flying a helicopter is one of the coolest, most exciting, activities ever! Imagine the scene. Your mates are all goofing around in the playground. Suddenly, a great clattering, screaming, ear-splitting roar comes from somewhere behind the dining hall. They look skywards. Moments later, a gigantic, shimmering, red-and-silver miracle of modern engineering thunders into view. It's you! In your brand-new chopper with integral infrared envy monitor and computer-controlled charisma launcher.

Your mates all gasp in disbelief and amazement. Hovering just a few metres above them, you smile down with a mixture of pity and scorn. You twitch your 'cyclic' – the lever that controls the 'attitude' of your chopper (see page 37) – you lower your 'collective', the one that controls its 'altitude' (see page 36). You go up. You go down. You go sideways. Then, as tears of envy and awe begin to trickle down the cheeks of the gobsmacked wimps you used to call your chums, you actually fly backwards! And finally, with inch-perfect precision, you land your beautiful chopper in the headteacher's parking spot. Cool or what?

Unfortunately, action-seeker, you can't just leap into a helicopter and flit off into the wide blue yonder. There are a few things you must know before you can enjoy the stunning, action-packed experiences that go with flying these amazing machines. Like how to actually *fly* it. And how to deal with tricky situations such as a mid-air fire, or a crash-landing in the sea. And what to do if you're asked to get people off a sinking ship. And how to pursue a bunch of bank robbers in their getaway car. Your Action-Seeker Handbook will tell you all this, and tons of other useful stuff besides. In it, you will discover how your helicopter works; how to survive that ditching in the sea; how to speak 'helicopter'; how you can use your helicopter to save people's lives; and how a plastic spoon can help save *your* life! So what are you waiting for? Get your flame-proof flying suit on, bung on your 'bone-dome', rev up your chopper, and transform yourself into a helicopter pilot action-seeker!

How to ...
get started

TOP SECRET

HELICOPTER HAZARDS

Before you even meet your brilliant new flying machine, you need to be aware of all the hazards that go with being around helicopters. This is absolutely essential, as helicopters are very dangerous creatures and you must always, always, treat them with respect. Your helicopter has got at least 1,000 moving parts and many of them are desperate to kebab/fry/slice/barbecue the most delicate and useful bits of your body just when you're least expecting it.

The really dangerous bits

One – the main rotors
The main rotors of your helicopter spin about 500 times every minute. That means their tips are whizzing through the air 200 metres every single second. Fortunately for you, when your helicopter is parked on level ground the rotors are higher up than you are and won't decapitate you while they're whizzing around (unless you happen to be really tall).

WARNING
Never approach your helicopter when the rotors are spinning really, really slowly. This is when they are at their most droopy and it would be easy to get hit by a rotor tip.

Two – the tail rotor

The tail rotor is at the back end of your helicopter. It spins at a speed of about 200 metres every second and it's also low to the ground. It's impossible to see the rotor when it's spinning. And it's even *more* impossible to see when it's spinning at night. So always always approach your helicopter from the front end. Most accidents associated with helicopters on the ground happen when people's heads come into contact with tail rotors that they've not noticed. Ouch!

If, for some reason, you do have to walk around the tail section of your helicopter, give it a very wide berth (anywhere between 12 metres and 25 kilometres).

Heli-snippet

Some helicopters have no tail rotors. They are known as 'NOTARs' which stands for No Tail Rotor. Exhaust gases from the helicopter's jet engine are used to counteract 'torque' (see page 31) as well as to steer the helicopter. These exhaust gases are seriously hot so, if your head comes anywhere near them, it won't be diced or kebabbed ... it will be grilled instead.

MAKING FRIENDS WITH YOUR CHOPPER

1 Always approach your helicopter as if you're a medieval peasant about to confess to Attila the Hun that you've just accidentally barbecued his favourite horse.

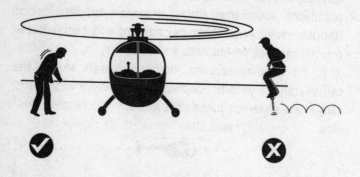

2 Never ever run when you're around a helicopter. You may have noticed TV celebrities regularly running to and from their helicopters. But they're just being dimwit posers and it's definitely *not* a good idea. You wouldn't believe the amount of celebs TV companies get through (which isn't a problem as they have warehouses full of doubles – but there's only *one* of you).

3 If you're wearing a helmet, woolly hat, baseball cap, pretend antlers, or any other sort of headgear, make sure you fasten it to your head securely. Failing that, just whip it off and stuff it inside your shirt. Three-metre-long scarves, wigs and pet parrots are particularly vulnerable to being sucked up into helicopter rotor blades.

4 Put goggles on to protect your eyes from the 'rotor wash' (the massive great draught that the rotor blades cause when they're spinning). It will pick up any loose objects or bits of dirt that happen to be lying around, then fling them towards anyone who happens to be standing near by. At heliports, the people in charge make sure that landing areas are kept clear of loose material at all times by sweeping them regularly and wetting them down. However, landings and takeoffs at other, wilder, places are frequently subject to flying dust, stones, branches (and the odd stray moose or grizzly bear).

Heli-snippet

At one heliport, a chopper made a bad landing and bits of debris flew off in all directions. A member of the ground crew stuck his head out of his caravan to see what all the noise was about and was instantly killed by a chunk of broken rotor blade. He was 150 metres away from the helicopter.

5 If you have them, wear earplugs. The noise from the helicopter's engine is quite deafening and you must protect your delicate hearing organs from it.

6 When you approach your helicopter, your co-pilot may well already be sitting at the controls, having kindly decided to do the necessary safety checks and start up the engine for you. If they are, wait for a thumbs up (or suggestive wink) from them before making your way towards your chopper. Don't approach it without their permission. If it looks like they're ignoring you, they aren't. They know exactly where you are but don't want to make contact until the exactly the right moment.

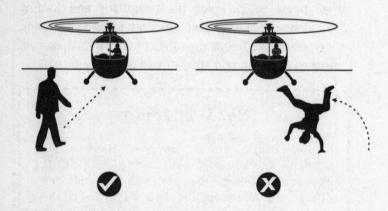

A word about 'heli-petting'

No matter how deeply you finally fall in love with your wondrous new helicopter never *ever* stroke, fondle or even snog it. Although it can be very tempting, you must not touch any part of the helicopter other than the bits that are designed to be pulled, pressed and tweaked. It has many fragile parts that could be damaged.

HAVE YOU BEEN
PAYING ATTENTION?

1 You must always treat your helicopter ...

a) with really strong cough mixture.

b) to a slap-up cream tea.

c) with respect.

2 A helicopter without a tail rotor is referred to as ...

a) a NUTTER.

b) a NOTAR.

c) sad.

3 Rotor wash is ...

a) what pilots give their choppers on Sunday mornings.

b) a cross between a power shower and a merry-go-round.

c) the down draught from a helicopter's rotor blades.

4 Most helicopters ...

a) are held together with string and wallpaper paste.

b) have at least 1,000 moving parts.

c) can't remain airborne for longer than three minutes.

YOUR CHOPPER UP CLOSE

Rotor hub

Rotor shaft

Windows (for good all-round visibility)

Cockpit

Wire snipper

Cabin door

Skids

Heli-basket
Used to lift whole groups of people into the helicopter.

Winch
Used on search and rescue helicopters to lower rescuers and their equipment to people in trouble.

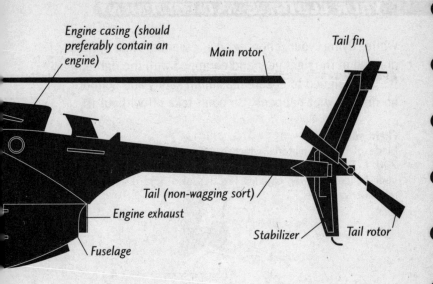

Engine casing (should preferably contain an engine)

Main rotor

Tail fin

Tail (non-wagging sort)

Engine exhaust

Fuselage

Stabilizer

Tail rotor

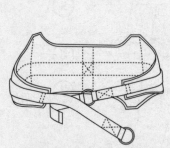

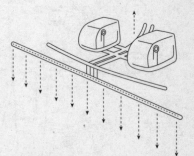

Rescue strop
Used to lift individual people up into the helicopter (or for dangling stroppy people over lakes full of crocodiles).

Spraying gear
Attached to helicopter when spraying crops to destroy bugs and diseases (or for fixing really big hairdos).

YOUR CLOTHING AND EQUIPMENT

While flying your chopper it's essential that you're dressed in the right gear and equipped with the right kit. It's all designed to ensure maximum safety and comfort, no matter what happens. So don't take off without it!

Flight suit
Made of Nomex material which can resist heat and fire up to 700° F. This fireproof flying suit will protect you against burns if your helicopter ever catches fire. It's also acid resistant and machine washable.

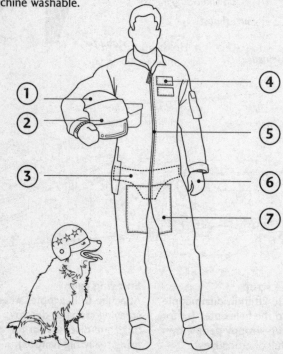

① Helmet (or your 'bone-dome' as you helicopter pilots call it). Strong, comfortable and light.

② Visor to prevent glare and protect your face in a crash.

③ Undies made of cotton so they won't melt and stick to you if your chopper catches fire. (Ouch!)

④ Velcro tabs ... to stick your badges on.

⑤ Specially designed zip fasteners won't reflect on your flying instruments during night flights.

⑥ Flight gloves made of Nomex.

⑦ Two handy upper-thigh openings so you can go to the loo without leaving your seat.

Kneeboard
Strap it to your thigh. Holds your flight chart (map), checklists, flight information – all conveniently at your fingertips.

Snazzy silver wings logo. (Hmm, nice!)

Holders for your small flight computer, pens and torch

Thin clipboard which won't get in the way of your helicopter's flight controls

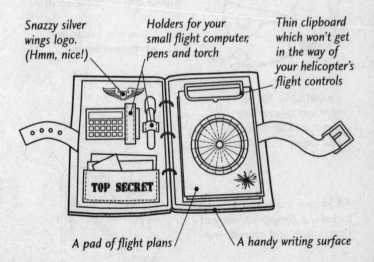

A pad of flight plans

A handy writing surface

Cockpit flight bag

To carry and protect your flight
helmet, flying gear, sandwiches,
toothbrush and toothpaste.

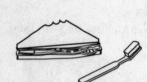

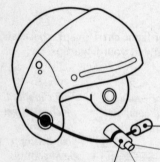

Radio headset

Used to communicate with your
co-pilot and air-traffic control.

*Convenient hands-free
microphone boom*

*Liplight which fits on
your microphone boom
and you switch it on with
your tongue*

All-in-one multi-purpose tool

Includes a dangerous array of
saws, knives and screwdrivers.

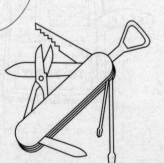

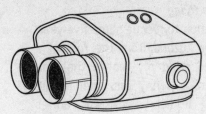

Night-vision goggles
Forget carrots, just put these on and you can see in the dark.

Pilot sunglasses
Strong and comfortable, they stop you being blinded when flying towards the sun.

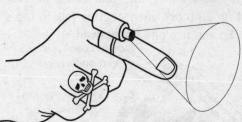

Fingerlight ring
Fits on your finger for reading maps and manuals in the dark.

First-aid kit
For use inside and outside your helicopter.

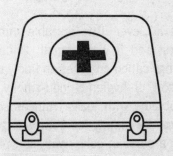

Survival kit
See page 41.

Going to the loo when you're flying

It's no good being on a mission to rescue some five-year-old orphans and their new kittens from the roof of a burning Toys R Us only to suddenly realize that you desperately need to spend a penny and then waste valuable seconds hovering above busy town centres frantically looking for somewhere to have a tiddle, not to mention a convenient parking space to go with it. So what do you do? Well, you certainly don't ask your co-pilot to take over the controls while you have a swift wee out of your 'copter's door or window. Not only is that not *nice*, but it's also unhygienic and could be extremely unpleasant for all those unsuspecting folk in the streets below you. So you use one of these:

It's a clever little portable mini-toilet gizmo. It won't burst and it won't smell. Once you've tiddled into it, things called enzymes and polymers turn your tiddle into a sort of hygienic, non-smelly jelly so there'll be no problems with leaks. And as soon as you get back to base you simply lob your wee parcel in the wee'ly bin! It's a piece of cake (well, sort of).

BUILDING YOUR OWN HELIPAD

As an action-seeking helicopter pilot you'll obviously need somewhere to land your helicopter. Many pilots use the local airfield; however, if you've got a big garden, well away from neighbours' houses, that will be just perfect. You don't always need planning permission or a licence to fly your helicopter in or out of it. All you have to do is build yourself a handy helipad, then flit here and there as you please: a swift trip to school; a flight over the traffic jams to feel all smug and superior; a jaunt to the shops; a day trip to Silverstone to see the British Grand Prix – it's all a simple matter of jumping in your chopper and away you go (certainly beats standing in the rain waiting for the bus which never arrives).

What you need:

a) Some yellow and white paint.

b) A big paintbrush.

c) A tall pole.

d) A large, bright-orange windsock.

e) A level piece of ground – preferably not boggy as you don't both want to be disappearing without a trace on rainy days. Good grass or a solid surface is best.

What to do:

1 Map out the diameter of your helipad. It should be about 35 metres across, although 20 metres will be enough if you've got a small, single-engined helicopter.

2 Work out your approach paths to your helipad. That's the various directions you'll fly in from. They need to be clear of obstructions like buildings, power lines, tall trees (and 25-metre-tall gorillas).

Action-Seeker Tip

If there is an airfield close to your garden, you should check with local air-traffic control to see if you're going to be getting in the way of other aircraft. You don't want to suddenly find yourself in the flight-path of a jet travelling at 500 mph.

3 Paint a large white 'H' in the middle of your landing area. Resist the temptation to paint the initial letter of your name instead (unless of course, your name's Harry or Helen). It will look rather like rugby goalposts that have fallen over (so watch out for short-sighted rugby players).

4 Now paint a yellow circle around the H. The radius of this circle must be at least half the overall length of your helicopter.

5 Stick a tall pole in the ground near to your circle but not so near that you're likely to fly smack into it when you're landing. Now tie a windsock to the pole. This is essential as you need to know the wind direction and strength for takeoffs and landings. Windsocks are available at all good aviation supply outlets.

6 If you're thinking of taking off and landing at night you'll have to light up your helipad. Set some lights in the surrounding ground to outline its shape, then put up some powerful floodlights in the area beyond that.

7 Keep some fire extinguishers and a water hose near your helipad in case your chopper suddenly bursts into flames on landing.

Heli-snippet

Why are helicopters called helicopters? We get the word from the Greek 'helix' which means spiral and 'pteron' which means wing. So, technically speaking, the helicopter ought to be called the helixpteron. However, it's much easier to say, 'Help, we need to be rescued. Send for the helicopter!' rather than, 'Help, we need to be rescued! Send for the the hxplitrer ... the hexteri ... the hippoter... Oh cripes ... glug glug glug...' Which may be why it ended up getting called what it did.

HAVE YOU BEEN
PAYING ATTENTION?

1 A winch is ...
a) a cheery, rosy-cheeked girl often seen serving cider in ye olde taverns.
b) a mechanical device used for lowering and raising a cable from a helicopter.
c) something people do if they aren't happy.

2 The most convenient and hygienic way to go the loo when you're flying is ...
a) out of the window.
b) in a portable throwaway mini loo.
c) in the great big potty under your seat.

3 Quite close to your helipad you should always put up a bright-orange ...
a) windsock.
b) windbag.
c) wind chime.

How to ...
take flight

THE BASIC IDEA

The secret of flying is the wing or, as techno-warriors like to call it, the 'aerofoil'.

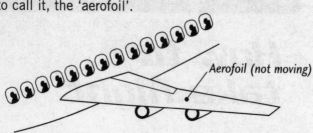

Aerofoil *(not moving)*

The principle is quite simple. If this wing thing is moving forwards through the air, some of the air flows *underneath* it and some of the air flows *over the top* of it. Because of the wing's unique shape, the amount of air flowing over the top of it is faster than that flowing underneath it.

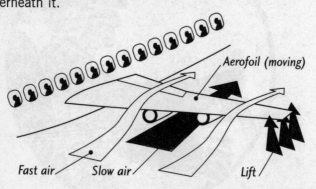

Aerofoil *(moving)*

Fast air   *Slow air*   *Lift*

Faster air causes lower pressure and slower air causes high pressure. Air always goes from high to low pressure, therefore this 'inequality of pressure' has the effect of forcing the wing up into the air or creating what is generally known as 'lift' by people in the aviation business. If this magic lift effect is powerful enough, whatever is attached to that wing (or wings), e.g. a long metal tube stuffed with smiling cabin stewards and people in garish leisurewear ... will rise up with it.

Aeroplanes are divided into two main sorts:

a) Fixed-wing aircraft.

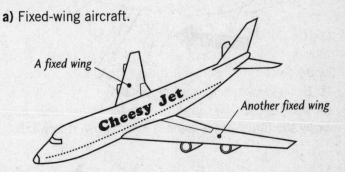

A fixed wing

Cheesy Jet

Another fixed wing

b) Rotary-wing aircraft – in other words the type that rescues children who have been swept out to sea on inflatable crocodiles.

In order for lift to occur, the all-important aerofoil has to keep moving forwards. On fixed-wing aircraft, this forward movement is created either by a propeller that *pulls* the aeroplane along ...

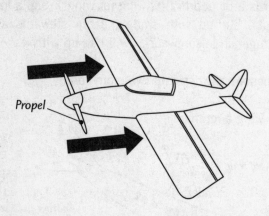

Propel

or by the thrust of jet engines which *push* it forwards.

Thrust

An easier way to make a wing move forwards is to spin it. In order to do this, you fasten two or more wings to a central stick-shaped thing known as a shaft, then you rotate it.

This wing-on-a-stick arrangement is known as a rotary wing because it rotates.

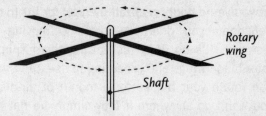

Rotary wing

Shaft

A rotary-winged aircraft is commonly called a helicopter (and should not be mistaken for a ceiling fan). A helicopter's wings are attached to a rotating column (or shaft) which pokes through its roof. They're shaped just like the aerofoils of an aeroplane's wing, but are much narrower and thinner because they must spin really quickly. Bulkier, heavier aerofoils aren't suited to whizzing around really fast.

The rotating wing assembly on a helicopter is normally referred to as its main rotor and it's usually powered by a petrol engine or a gas turbine engine (or, if it's a really cheap helicopter, a giant elastic band).

The engine drives the rotor shaft, and the efficient operation of this assembly, and consequently your safety, all depends on one thing: your Jesus nut – the nut that holds your rotor hub assembly on to the shaft.

Pilots joke that if it ever drops off, the next person you see will be Jesus.

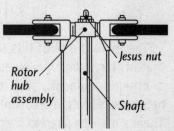

Jesus nut

Rotor hub assembly

Shaft

BECOMING AIRBORNE

As you've no doubt realized by now, for lift to occur in a helicopter you don't need to be moving forwards. However, it's no good just sitting there spinning your rotor-blade wings and expecting to rise up in the air. You can rotate your blades for a month of air-displays but you won't go anywhere if they simply lie flat. You must give them what is known as an 'angle of attack' or 'pitch'. In other words, you must *tilt* all your rotor blades at the same time. To do this you have a special device called a collective pitch control, which you can read more about on page 36. Raising your collective pitch control causes the front of the blades to go up like this.

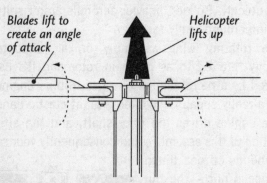

Blades lift to create an angle of attack

Helicopter lifts up

The more the front tilts the more your rotors develop that lift force which is so essential for takeoff. Then, at a critical moment, your rotor lift will exceed your helicopter's weight and up you will go. Well, almost. There's a slight snag to overcome first...

A short talk about torque

While your helicopter is in contact with the ground, it's all fine and dandy to be spinning your wing-on-a-stick rotor assembly. However, the moment you lose contact with the ground, your helicopter's body will begin whizzing around in the opposite direction. This is known as the 'torque effect'.

Fortunately though, the people who make helicopters have already thought of this. To keep the helicopter's body from spinning they've fixed a second rotor on the end of your chopper's tail. It sits vertically on the tail and spins in the opposite direction to your main rotor.

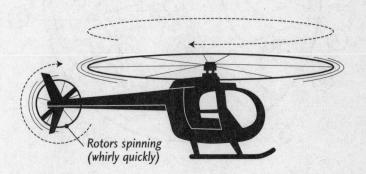

Rotors spinning
(whirly quickly)

This opposite force keeps the body of the helicopter from spinning. And what's more, not only does this clever device prevent the dreaded torque effect from happening, but it can also be used to balance your helicopter when it's flying.

MAKING YOURSELF AT HOME IN YOUR COCKPIT

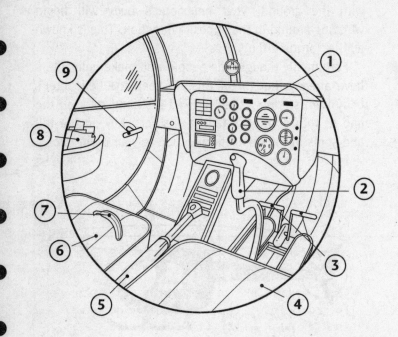

1. Control panel (see opposite diagram)
2. Cyclic pitch lever
3. Foot pedals
4. Your seat
5. Collective pitch lever
6. Co-pilot's seat
7. Snack
8. Maps
9. Door lever

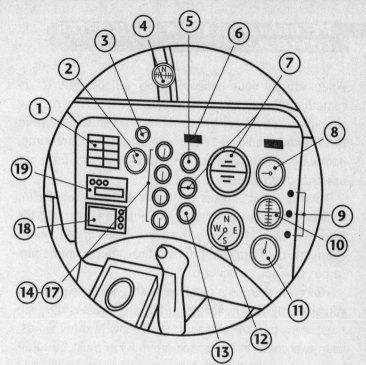

1. **Warning panel –**
   fire, high temps etc
2. **Fuel gauge**
3. **Stop-watch**
4. **Standby compass**
5. **Airspeed**
   indicator (knots)
6. **Warning lights**
7. **Attitude indicators**
8. **Altimeter**
9. **Dimmers for**
   instrument lights
10. **Hover indicator**
    (perfect cross when
    perfect hover)
11. **Rate of climb or**
    descent indicator
12. **Directional gyro**
13. **Torque and**
    rotor RPM indicator
14. **Engine temp**
15. **Gearbox temp**
16. **Engine oil**
    pressure
17. **Gear oil**
    pressure
18. **GPS (global**
    positioning system)
19. **VHF radio**

RECOGNIZING YOUR HELICOPTER CONTROLS

When you fly your helicopter you will be able to do something that most humans (apart from gravity-defying astronauts) never get to do. You will be able to move in *three* dimensions! In other words not only forwards, backwards, sideways (as you do on the ground), but upwards and downwards too!

This is what makes helicopters such wonderful, brilliant and unique machines, enabling them to fly, land and take off from almost anywhere in the world. (All right, *not* from that little cupboard under your stairs ... but now you're being picky!)

However, there is a catch to all this wonderfulness. If you are to fly your helicopter safely and successfully, you must learn to *think* three dimensionally. In other words, your awareness of the space around you must be total! If it isn't you will soon find yourself zooming up into power lines or down onto the roofs of passing double-decker buses.

In order not to get you too confused (or reduce you to floods of tears) all of the instructions below are generally for a single main rotor, piston-engine helicopter. That's the sort with the horizontal rotor blades on top and another (vertical one) on the tail, both of which are driven by a petrol engine.

You've got four main helicopter controls. They are called:

a) Your collective pitch lever
b) Your cyclic pitch lever
c) Your right anti-torque pedal
d) Your left anti-torque pedal

Action-Seeker Tip

Do not panic midway through your first flight when you suddenly discover that someone has removed the steering wheel from your aircraft. Helicopters do not have steering wheels.

In order to operate your four controls, you use both of your hands and both of your feet at the same time – preferably with your feet on the pedals and your hands on the control levers.

This is not an easy thing to do and requires lots of smooth and totally focussed coordination. Therefore, if you are the sort of person who: **a)** is not yet confident enough to have your stabilizers removed from your bicycle; and **b)** has difficulty watching the TV and eating a soft-centred chocolate at the same time, you might well not be best suited to becoming a helicopter pilot.

Flying a helicopter is a tiring and demanding activity during which you can't let your concentration slip for one moment. As a result, helicopter pilots always have lots and lots of sleep (but not normally while they're flying).

Your collective pitch lever

Sometimes just known as your *collective*, this is operated with your *left* hand. You are already familiar with the idea of your rotor blades all needing to have collective pitch in order for you to create lift. Well, it's your *collective* that changes the angle of attack, or pitch, of your main rotor blades. But that's not all your collective does. It also has a throttle on it, which controls the helicopter's speed.

Your throttle control

This is mounted on your collective pitch lever so that you can use the two of them in a controlled and coordinated way. Your throttle feeds fuel to your engine and therefore increases the RPM (revolutions per minute) of your rotor. It makes your main rotor blade spin round faster or slower, depending on how much welly* you give it. (*Highly technical aviation term, far too complex to explain here.)

As you increase your collective pitch, you must give your throttle some more welly so that your rotor blades are spinning around fast enough and therefore providing enough power for your helicopter to rise upwards.

Your cyclic pitch lever

As you sit in your cockpit, your cyclic pitch lever, or cyclic, sticks up between your legs. You operate your cyclic with the hand that isn't operating the collective – in other words, your right hand. You use your cyclic to control all the *lateral* directions your helicopter moves in. In other words, forwards, backwards, left and right.

Like your collective, your cyclic controls the angle of attack or pitch of your rotor blades. But, unlike your collective, it changes the pitch of the rotor blades individually and not collectively, by tilting your rotor disc. Your rotor will tilt your helicopter in the direction that you apply pressure to your cyclic pitch control.

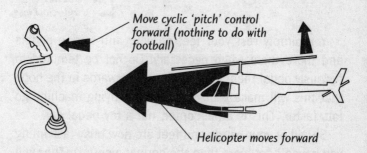

Move cyclic 'pitch' control forward (nothing to do with football)

Helicopter moves forward

In other words, you use your cyclic for controlling precise movements in flight rather than achieving lift-off.

Your anti-torque pedals

Your two anti-torque pedals counteract torque by providing a means of changing the angle of attack, or pitch, of the tail rotor blades. As a result, moving the pedals forwards and backwards will allow you to control the direction of your helicopter while you're hovering *and* while you're flying at relatively slow airspeeds. As you operate them they cause your helicopter to rotate on its axis in either direction.

Like this:

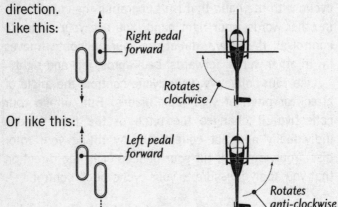

Right pedal
forward

Rotates
clockwise

Or like this:

Left pedal
forward

Rotates
anti-clockwise

You simply rest your feet on your anti-torque pedals and move them when necessary. Do not be tempted to furiously pedal them backwards and forwards in the hope that this will make your rotary-winged flying machine go lots faster. This is a helicopter, not a toy pedal car.

So, all of your hands and feet are now busy (assuming you haven't got more than the normal amount). They will stay that way for your entire flight (and will possibly carry on pedalling and pulling in your sleep).

Action-Seeker Tip

While flying your chopper, always remember to move your controls *carefully* and *smooooothly*, finely adjusting them a bit here and a bit there. And no matter how excited you are feeling, please refrain from behaving like a baby chimpanzee that's just been let loose in an amusement arcade. Certainly never attempt to jerk, wrench, force, chew or even to *suck* your cockpit controls.

HAVE YOU BEEN PAYING ATTENTION?

1 Your cyclic pitch control lever ...

a) operates the cigar lighter.

b) is there to hang your jacket on.

c) controls the lateral direction of the helicopter.

2 You operate your collective pitch lever with ...

a) your right armpit.

b) your left hand.

c) your right hand.

3 Your throttle control is mounted ...

a) on a seaside donkey called Ned.

b) on your collective pitch lever.

c) and stuffed.

FLYING SAFELY

Helicopters are miraculous machines capable of performing all sorts of stunning stunts and feats. However, if not handled properly, they are also incredibly dangerous and a thousand and one different sorts of accidents await the action-seeker who ignores basic safety rules. In order to ensure that the action-packed hours you spend in your chopper are risk-free, you must familiarize yourself with safe flying procedures and learn how to deal with some of the many dangerous and challenging situations you'll be bound to come across when you're piloting your chopper.

Before you take off

1 Once you're suited and booted (pilot-speak for having your flying kit on), the first thing you must do is walk around your helicopter and closely look at all the parts to make sure they're undamaged and in the right places. If you do find something that looks as if it's not quite right (e.g. main rotor blades missing) you mustn't fly under any circumstances (not that you'd be able to if the rotor blades *were* missing).

2 Don't just flit off into the wild blue yonder without telling a soul where you're going. Discuss your flight plan with people. Tell your team members, friends (and your mum) where you're headed. Brief them (that's a different way of saying 'tell them') on what to do if you're late – things like: **a)** alerting local coast guards; **b)** calling out search teams; and **c)** and putting your dinner in the oven until you're rescued.

3 Check the weather forecast. Storms can blow up out of nowhere and can be really dangerous once you're up in the air (see page 97).

4 Make sure you've got your emergency kit with you in case you do have to come down in a dangerous out-of-the-way spot and have a long wait before you're rescued or make your way back to civilization. Here are some of the things you might include in your emergency survival kit:

a) Survival manual packed full of tips on staying alive.

b) Whistle to alert search rescuers to your position.

c) Signal mirror. A simple mirror can be seen by rescuers up to 100 miles away. And of course, your mirror will also come in handy for smartening yourself up a bit before you're rescued. You don't want your rescuers thinking you're some sort of scruff-bag layabout.

d) Strobe light for attracting the attention of would-be rescuers (or wandering disco freaks). A 360° high intensity strobe can be seen for many kilometres.

e) Flares. Special devices designed to attract the attention of rescuers, not the wide-bottomed fashion trousers (they're utterly useless as a survival aid unless you set fire to them or wave them around your head).

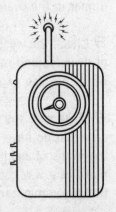

f) EPIRB (Emergency Position Indicating Radio Beacon) to help rescuers find you wherever you've crashed.

g) Space blanket (one per person) for keeping warm.

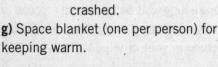

h) First-aid kit for repairing yourself or your crew.

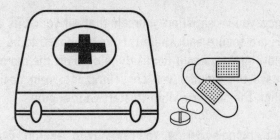

i) Food (two days' emergency rations per person).

j) 1.5 litres of water per person to be used sparingly.

k) Water purification tablets.

l) Collapsible water bag.

m) Stainless-steel drinking cup.

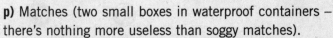

 **n)** Nylon rope (20 metres) and snare wire.

o) Fishhooks and snare line.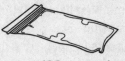

p) Matches (two small boxes in waterproof containers – there's nothing more useless than soggy matches).

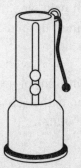 **q)** Watertight electric torch for finding things in the dark (and playing that game where you make horrid faces to scare the life out of your pals).

r) Spare torch batteries and bulb in case you're lost for a long time (hopefully not!).

... and a partridge in a pear tree (optional).

Taking off

1 Once you've satisfied yourself that all your bits and pieces are secure and where they're supposed to be and that nothing looks as if it's likely to drop off the moment you leave the ground, you can climb into your cockpit and flick the starter switch to start your engine.

2 Your engine's roaring. You're ready to take off. Good! Now, make a mental note of a reference point that is at least 15–23 metres away from you. For instance, something like a tall building or a big tree (but not a speeding train or galloping pony).

When you finally lift off you must use that point and the horizon as references to help you stay lined up and to gauge your height from the ground.

3 Don't stare at the bit of ground just in front of your helicopter's nose. It will distract you from the job in hand (apart from which, it's really quite boring).

4 Set your cyclic in a neutral position.

5 Set your collective full down and use your throttle to increase your RPM.

6 Once you've established the proper operating RPM for takeoff, raise your collective and steadily increase your RPM as you do so.

7 Depending on things like your helicopter's weight, the wind conditions (and what you had for lunch today) your helicopter should become 'light on its skids'. In other words, the effects of gravity will lessen and the entire chopper will feel less heavy and less like it's glued to the ground.

8 You are finally about to take leave of the ground (or your senses).

9 Because you're creating extra torque by increasing the pitch of your helicopter's main rotor blades you will now feel your helicopter trying to turn to the left or right. DON'T LET IT! You must let your chopper know that *you* are the boss. If it senses that you are feeling the least bit of fear or uncertainty it will become dominant and aggressive.

10 Now, as your helicopter attempts to turn to the left or right, use your anti-torque pedals to stay pointing in the direction you wish to go. Otherwise you may find yourself flying to Brussels, which could be really irritating if you'd planned on spending an afternoon in Belfast.

11 At this point, your cyclic will become really sensitive (so avoid sneering at it — sticks have feelings too you know). But, more to the point, this is the stunning, heart-stopping, suddenly-desperate-to-visit-the-toilet-for-at-least-the-entire-afternoon moment when your helicopter will slowly and majestically begin to rise into the air (or fall to pieces).

12 At the moment you feel your helicopter leaving the ground, remember to make sure you remain calm, focussed and confident, and *smooothly* move your cyclic forward. This will have the effect of making both you, your helicopter (and your cyclic) move forward too.

13 As your helicopter moves forward, it will begin to speed up until you're doing about 15 knots (approx 24 km/h). At this point your chopper will give a little shudder. That's right, it's just as excited as you are! Actually, that's not true, the reason it shudders is because you're moving into something called ETL (Effective Translational Lift) and your helicopter is leaving the 'cushion-of-ground effect'. In other words, the further away from the ground you are, the less your helicopter will be affected by the interaction between the air currents created by your rotor blades and the ground itself.

You will now enter what is known to your fellow action-seeking heli-pilots as 'clean air' and your cyclic will try to move backward in your hand. DON'T ALLOW IT TO DO THIS! Keep steadily pushing it forward.

14 By moving through ETL you are simply going from 'hover' mode to 'forward flight' mode. You must now ease off the pressure on both your collective and your anti-torque pedals, but continue to smoothly push your cyclic forward to counteract the air pressure forces that are building up against the front of the rotor system.

If you do *not* do this, the following things will happen:

a) the nose of your helicopter will suddenly point upwards rather than downwards (as it should be doing);

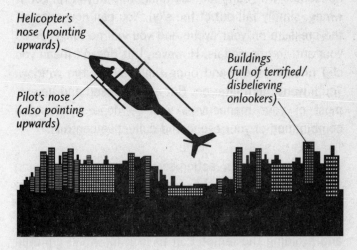

Helicopter's nose (pointing upwards)

Pilot's nose (also pointing upwards)

Buildings (full of terrified/ disbelieving onlookers)

b) your forward speed will reduce drastically; and
c) a large crowd of helicopter pilots, mechanics and really cool people will gather alongside the takeoff area and begin pointing, laughing and jeering at you. And you don't want that to happen, do you?

15 So! Got that cyclic pushed well forward? Good! Now, having felt that special ETL shudder, you will begin to notice an increase in your forward airspeed. This means that your rotor system is now becoming more and more effective. You can therefore reduce the pressure on your anti-torque pedals and your collective even further and your airspeed indicator will now jump from zero to at least 40 knots.

16 Your airspeed will continue to increase and the helicopter will carry on climbing (or, if you've got it wrong, simply fall out of the sky). You can now ease off the pressure on your cyclic and you will no longer need your anti-torque pedals. However, this doesn't mean you can unscrew them and bung them out of the window. You'll want them later on. But at this speed and height, most of your manoeuvres will be done by using a combination of your cyclic and collective controls.

17 Congratulations, action-seeker! You are now flying your helicopter for the first time (or being given emergency first aid at the side of a field). Please fly carefully, observing speed limits through built-up areas and avoiding the temptation to look for small children on bikes so that you can race them.

How to ... take flight

How to ... take flight

Golden rule of flying

While you're flying, try to stay in the middle of the air. In other words, stay well away from the edges. You will recognize the edges by tell-tale clues such as the appearance of things like supermarkets, schools, sea, fields, trees and interstellar space. It is much more difficult to fly safely in these places.

Flying your chopper straight and level

This is the normal way of flying a helicopter when you want to get from one place to another. When you do it, you fly at a constant speed, altitude and heading (direction). Here's what to do:

1 Climb to at least 150 metres. Your altimeter will tell you what height you're flying at.

2 Keep your altitude steady and constant by raising or lowering your collective as necessary.

3 As you raise and lower your collective, use your anti-torque pedals to keep your flight coordinated. So, if you want to add power, push your left pedal. And if you want to decrease power, push your right pedal.

4 Use your cyclic to keep your chopper level.

5 If the wind is making your chopper drift a bit, use your anti-torque pedals to turn your helicopter slightly into the wind. This will keep you on course.

6 Remember to coordinate the use of your controls. Moving one of them usually requires you to move another.

Hovering

Hovering is flying your helicopter so that it remains in a constant position at a constant height above the ground. It's the main thing that choppers can do and fixed-wing aircraft can't. However, it's not easy. This is because helicopters are naturally unstable (aaah!). Without you tweaking your columns and pumping your pedals, they flop and roll all over the place (and if you're not all that good at it, they'll probably do that anyway). When things like bad weather in the form of sharp updraughts of air and unexpected gusts of wind come along, your helicopter's lack of inherent stability becomes particularly noticeable. This is why you must learn to master your controls to the point where you could fly your helicopter in your sleep (but preferably not). It's also why hovering your chopper is one of the most difficult manoeuvres you'll ever learn to master.

So you can forget all about manoeuvring into a hovering position above a football stadium, getting out your sandwiches and fizzy drinks and sitting back to enjoy the match. To stay at the same height and position above the ground you must be constantly moving your cyclic, your collective and your anti-torque pedals. If you fail to do this, even for a second or two, you'll immediately lose control of your aircraft.

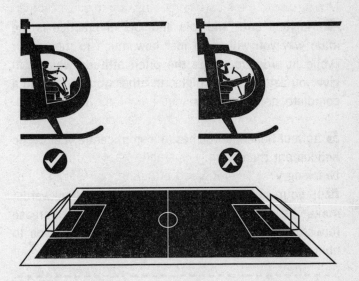

Here's how to do it:

1 Climb to the position you intend to hover at, using your collective control to adjust your height. This is the relatively easy part of this manoeuvre. Now for the tricky bit!

2 When you're more or less in position, look out the window and decide exactly where you want to hover in relation to a spot on the ground below you.

3 Now move your cyclic to gain this position. Remember, moving your cyclic affects the speed, attitude and position of your chopper, so, if you want to be a bit to the right of your immediate position, move your cyclic to the right.

4 Trial and error and lots and lots of practice is the main way you will learn just how much to move your cyclic in order to create the pitch attitude which will give you zero airspeed flight. In other words, come to a complete stop in mid-air.

5 As your helicopter comes to a stop, centre your cyclic and keep it there.

6 If your helicopter drifts forwards or backwards, make little changes with your cyclic to increase forwards or backwards speed. This will enable you to hold your hover.

Heli-snippet

In 1989, a chopper beat the world helicopter hovering record when it was kept in the air for more than 50 hours. Four pilots took turns to keep it aloft in just one spot, swapping controls when they needed a rest.

Landing

Even if you find flying your chopper so brilliant and exciting that you never ever want to stop, you will still have to come down to earth at some point or other (but preferably not with a bump). Here's how to do it:

1 Decrease your power as you hover.

Action-Seeker Tip

While you're doing this don't look directly in front of your helicopter. You'll do loads better if you either look up at the horizon, or halfway between the ground in front of your helicopter and the horizon (i.e. a spot 15–30 metres in front of your chopper). It's really important to know where the horizon is at all times. If you look at areas too close to your helicopter you won't be able to see it.

2 You will now begin to descend. While you're doing this manoeuvre, don't look down to judge your height above the ground. Your 'peripheral' vision will do this for you (that's all the stuff you see on the edge of your field of vision).

3 As you go down, lower your collective to keep a steady descent rate. Don't let your descent speed exceed 92 metres per minute.

4 As you approach the ground, allow the 'cushion-of-ground effect' (see page 47) to slow down your descent rate for a softer landing. But don't stop coming down.

5 When the ground seems to be about level with your ears, it means that you're about to touch down (or that your ears have just fallen off).

6 One of your skids will now touch the ground. If your helicopter isn't hovering perfectly level, this will cause it to pitch or roll. If it does, move your cyclic in the opposite direction.

7 Balance for a few seconds, but don't let your helicopter drift around on the ground.

8 Lower the collective a bit more and put some more skid on the ground, while making up for any drifting movement by using your cyclic. Keep doing this a bit at a time until you have slowly lowered your chopper all the way on to the ground.

9 Well done, action-seeker, you're down. (Pity you've landed at the wrong heliport though.)

Mechanical problems during your flight

One of the huge advantages that helicopters have over fixed-wing aircraft is that they can land in thousands of places where the other sort can't. So if a helicopter pilot suspects they have a mechanical problem they can land at the first suitable spot and check out the fault. However, as a beginner, you should never attempt to take your helicopter to pieces after you've made an emergency landing in a field because you 'heard a funny knocking noise in that whirly bit on top', especially if you are not all that good at tinkering. Your helicopter is made up of thousands and thousands of very complicated bits and pieces and you may have difficulty putting it all back together again.

HAVE YOU BEEN PAYING ATTENTION?

1 In 1989 a helicopter was kept hovering for 50 hours ...

a) while the pilot looked for a parking space.

b) to break the world helicopter hovering record.

c) because the pilot hadn't the faintest idea how to land it.

2 ETL stands for …

a) Extra Terrestrial Loganberry.

b) Eric Thompson's Lughole.

c) Effective Translational Lift.

3 One of the many advantages that helicopters have over fixed-wing aircraft is that …

a) you can fold them up to the size of a postage stamp and keep them in your wallet.

b) they can land in all sorts of awkward spaces.

c) they're really faithful and brave and rarely make puddles on the kitchen floor.

4 As you're descending from a hover don't look …

a) a gift horse in the mouth.

b) down to judge your distance from the ground.

c) in other people's drawers.

How to ...
learn the
lingo

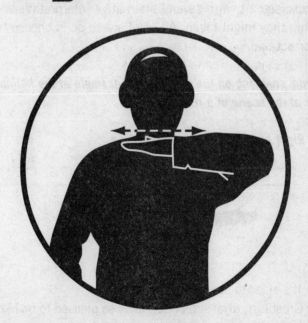

UNDERSTANDING HELICOPTER HAND SIGNALS

Because of the horrendous racket that your helicopter makes once you start up the engine you'll find it impossible to speak to people on the ground even if they're quite close or are trying to use some sort of two-way radio. In order to overcome this problem, a system of hand signals has been developed to enable pilots and people on the ground to communicate successfully. Here are some diagrams and descriptions of a few of these signals, with several alternative interpretations of what they might mean. All you have to do is choose the correct one.

From someone on the ground – for example at the helipad or at the scene of a rescue

1 Right hand making circular motion

a) It's clear to start your engine.
b) Greetings, royal subjects. One is so pleased to be here.
c) Your navigator's as nutty as a fruit bat.

2 Arms extended palms up and arms sweeping upwards

a) And when I do this I want you to sing four times louder.
b) No, I don't care what you say; it's definitely not raining!
c) Move upwards.

3 Arms held up with fists clenched

a) It's fair cop, I'll come quietly.
b) Hold hover.
c) I seem to have mixed up the superglue with my underarm deodorant.

4 Arms extended palms down and arms sweeping downwards

a) Phwoar ... it ain't half hot down here.
b) Move downwards.
c) I've been doing this for the last three days and I still haven't taken off.

5 Slash hand across throat

a) Don't look now, but there's an escaped maniac hiding under your helicopter.
b) Shut off your engine.
c) Don't come any closer, I don't want to give you my sore throat.

From someone in the water, i.e. the person you're rescuing

6 Raised arm – thumb up

a) Come on, don't be such a wimp – it's really warm once you're in.
b) I'm ready to be hoisted.
c) No, really. I really am fine. You lot just get off home and have your tea.

7 Raised arm clenched fist

a) Stop hoisting.
b) Power to the workers.
c) I've caught a fish! Would you believe it! I've caught a blinking fish!

8 Raised arm, thumb down

a) I think there's a shark biting my bum.
b) OK – lower the cable.
c) There seems to be a sea urchin thingy lodged in my left earhole.

From someone on the ground who looks like they might be in trouble

9 Arms raised, making body into a Y shape

a) Yes, I want to be rescued.
b) Oh my goodness, I seem to have turned into an oak tree.
c) Friends, Romans, countrymen ... lend me your ears.

10 One arm up at 45 degrees to body – other down at 45 degrees to body

a) So what do you think of my new outfit then?
b) No, I don't want to be rescued.
c) See, you aren't the only one who can do a banking turn.

THE PILOTS' ALPHABET

Because aircraft fly all over the world, and people all around the world speak different languages and pronounce things differently, something called the International Radio Alphabet has been invented to make for successful communication between pilots, air-traffic controllers (and transworld pizza delivery services).

For instance, if you wanted to tell a foreign radio operator that you were about to ditch in Lake Geneva and that your call sign (your unique aircraft 'registration' number) was ACTION SEEKER ONE you would say...

A for Alpha – **C** for Charlie – **T** for Tango – **I** for India – **O** for goodness' sake, pay attention, cloth-ears! for Oscar – **N** for November

S for Sierra – **E** for Echo – **E** for Echo – **K** for Kilo – **E** for Echo – **R** for Romeo

O for Oscar – **N** for November and **E** for Echo

... and they would hopefully get it right (or simply fall into a deep sleep).

So one of the things you must do is learn the following alphabet:

A lpha	**J** uliet	**S** ierra
B ravo	**K** ilo	**T** ango
C harlie	**L** ima	**U** niform
D elta	**M** ike	**V** ictor
E cho	**N** ovember	**W** hisky
F oxtrot	**O** scar	**X** -ray
G olf	**P** apa	**Y** ankee
H otel	**Q** uebec	**Z** ulu
I ndia	**R** omeo	

How to ...
cope with
heli-hazards

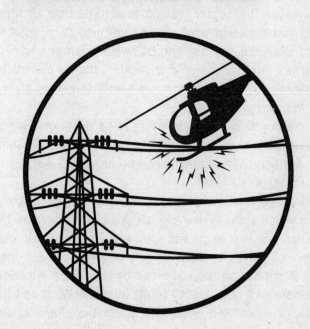

There's only one thing you can ever be sure of when you're flying. And that's that unexpected stuff will happen to you. Consequently, even the best chopper pilots get into situations that are both challenging and life-threatening. The best way to deal with them is to be prepared.

SURVIVING A CRASH IN WATER

During the various exciting, death-defying, action-packed adventures you're no doubt going to be having the moment you finish this book, you're bound to end up flying your helicopter over water at some time or other. Not just a garden pond containing three dead goldfish and a tadpole, but big, big, BIG water such as a lake, or the sea. And, whatever your mission, there's always the chance you might have to make an emergency landing in the water.

When you know you're going to be flying over water, you need to take the following emergency survival items in addition to those mentioned on pages 42–43:

a) Emergency life raft.

b) Emergency dye marker containing a fluorescent green dye which spreads over the surface of the water for the search-and-rescue crew to spot. Keep the marker in your life-vest pocket or your life-raft safety kit. The bright-green pattern on the water can be seen for a kilometre or more and lasts for 30 to 40 minutes. Wind and the choppiness of the water will affect the shape of the pattern. Make sure you don't accidentally puncture your dye marker whilst walking around with it in your pocket (or people may mistake you for a leek).

c) Floating throw ring with line to throw to other crew members or passengers in trouble in the water.

d) Floating anchors to keep your life raft away from danger areas and in the spot where rescuers expect to find you.

Throw this bit

Keep hold of this bit

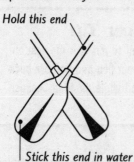

Hold this end

Stick this end in water

e) Bellows to pump up your life raft if it loses air.

f) Repair kit for repairing your life raft or life jacket.

g) Paddles for paddling towards land (or away from danger).

h) Bailer for scooping water out of your life raft.

i) Sponges for soaking up the last bits of water and keeping your raft clean.

Preparing for ditching

All sorts of difficulties may force you to bring down your chopper in the water: unforeseen technical problems; running out of fuel; horrendous weather; or maybe even sheer incompetence. Whatever the cause, you'll have to 'ditch', as it's known in the world of aviation. This doesn't mean that you must land in an actual ditch. This wouldn't be a very good idea as most ditches are nowhere near big enough to fit a full-size helicopter in. Here's what you must do if you know you're going to have to ditch:

1 If you're not already wearing it, put on your life vest and tell your passengers to do the same (that's put on their own life vests, not yours).

Action-Seeker Tip

You might have to undo your seat belt to put your life vest on. Whatever you do, don't forget to put your belt and harness back on before you ditch. People have died while ditching because they forgot to do this.

2 If you're wearing a tie, take it off. Also remove false teeth and fasten down any loose objects. Don't spend ages trying to take out the false teeth – you might not be wearing them ... especially if you're under 60.

3 Tuck any loose ends of your life-vest straps into your pocket or tie them up. These long loose ends can get caught up in your helicopter's equipment while you're scrambling out, leaving you trapped in the sinking aircraft.

Action-Seeker Tip

Never inflate your life vest until you're completely clear of your helicopter. Inflated life vests can make it difficult or even impossible to get out.

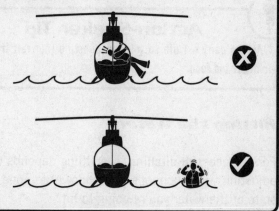

4 When you hit the water, the body of your chopper may be so badly bent that the doors are impossible to open without the aid of some cutting equipment or a chainsaw. In order to prepare for this possibility, either: **a)** unfasten the door(s) of your helicopter and jam something into the opening to stop them clicking shut again when you hit the water; or **b)** unfasten the door(s), then click the latch into locked position to prevent the doors slamming shut on impact. NB Some choppers have 'throwaway' doors. If your helicopter has them, unfasten them and throw them away (but be careful where you throw them).

5 In the chaos and confusion of ditching, your life raft could self-inflate inside the helicopter. Like the inflated life vests this could have the effect of trapping you in your sinking chopper.

Action-Seeker Tip

Always carry a knife so you can puncture your raft if it does inflate too soon.

Hitting the water

For a successful ditching, everything depends upon you adjusting your chopper's 'splashdown' to cope with the state of the water you're going to hit.

1 If you're ditching in a river, ditch by following the flow of the water, i.e. downstream. The water will be moving in the same direction as you so this will lower the speed at which you hit it.

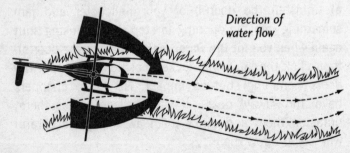

Direction of water flow

2 If you're ditching in a small or medium-sized lake, fly into the wind as you ditch. To work out which way the wind is blowing look at the way the frothy bits on top of the water are skittering across the lake.

Frothy bits (possibly bubble bath ... or fish spit)

3 If you're coming down in the sea (or a large lake), carry out the following procedure:

a) Try to work out which way the swells are moving. Swells are the long rounded parallel humps on the water's surface, which are caused by distant winds. You can see them really well if you're flying really high above the sea but the lower you fly, the more difficult it gets. So check them out while you're still high up.

b) Try to land along, or parallel to, a swell, not across it. If you land across the swell your impact on the water will be much, much harder.

4 Just before you hit the water, assume what is known as the 'crash position'. This will reduce the chances of you being seriously injured when the final impact takes place.

No matter what happens, stay like this until all forward motion of your chopper has stopped. Don't panic. It's easy to become disorientated by the water rushing in.

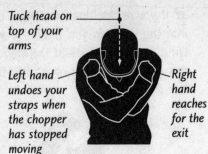

Tuck head on top of your arms

Left hand undoes your straps when the chopper has stopped moving

Right hand reaches for the exit

Some rather worrying information:

Once you've hit the water your helicopter will almost certainly sink before you can get out of it.

Some information that is even more worrying than the last bit:

Once you've hit the water your helicopter will almost certainly roll over and assume an upside-down position before you can get out of it.

Some really alarming information:

If the water is cold and your helicopter sinks really quickly, you will experience what is known as a 'cold-water-reflex'. Not just a little shiver and an uncontrollable urge to reach out and turn on the hot bath tap, but a terrible shock to your body immediately followed by an uncontrollable need to exhale (or 'breathe out', as experts say). No matter how hard you try to hold your breath the shock of suddenly being dunked in several quillion gallons of incredibly cold water will make you want to go, *Huuuuurgh! Aggggh! Jubba jubba jubba!* And obviously, the very thing you will need to be doing (unless you happen to have gills or are closely related to some porpoises) is actually holding your breath in order to stay alive.

Some information which may make you want to have a little weep:

Once your chopper has hit the water and rolled over things will get really frightening because:

a) tons of sea water will be rushing into your cockpit which only seconds earlier was warm and dry and cosy;

b) you will still be strapped into your seat;

c) you will be hanging upside down; and

d) it will be very dark if not to say pitch black.

As a result of all of these new sensations and circumstances you will become what is known as 'disorientated'. Or to put it more simply you won't know up from down, top from bottom, or left from right!

Getting out of a sinking helicopter

Once your helicopter's plunged into the water, sooner or later you're going to have to get out of it. Preferably sooner rather than later. However, there is one slight drawback to you making a quick getaway. You've got to wait for something called equalization-of-pressure to happen. This means that the water pressure on the inside of your chopper's doors must be equal to the water pressure on the outside. Otherwise, no matter how hard you push, the water pressure outside will stop you from opening them, even though you have unfastened them before hitting the water. And, for this equalization-of-pressure to happen, your helicopter's got to completely fill up with water. With you inside it! In other words you've got to sort of hang around while it happens, which can be a very scary time indeed. Here's what you must do to survive it:

1 Stay calm. There's time to get out, as long as you don't panic. You must now establish what is known as a 'reference point', i.e. something in the cockpit that is familiar to you. The door handle is probably best. Grab hold of it and keep holding it, no matter what.

2 You must now endure the agonizing wait while your cockpit fills with water. While you do, think your way through the escape procedure you're about to follow.

3 Now that the cockpit has filled with sea water you can open the door.

Action-Seeker Tip

If for some reason your doors won't open you can always try kicking out your helicopter's windows. Rest both your feet on the window with your knees bent, grab hold of something firm to brace yourself against and force your feet forwards with all your strength.

4 Grab the edge of the doorway and pull yourself through.

Action-Seeker Tip

Don't kick yourself free of your chopper! Unless you've been flying on your own, someone is likely to be right behind you and you don't want to end up kicking out your co-pilot's front teeth.

5 Once you're clear of your helicopter, obviously you must get to the surface of the water as quickly as you can. If your life vest hasn't inflated properly (or you aren't wearing one) blow a little air out of your mouth and follow the bubbles to the top – they will lead you to the surface.

6 As you rise to the surface breathe out *slooowly* and raise a hand (preferably your own) above your head. This will stop you crashing headfirst into something dangerous like a section of your helicopter or perhaps even puncturing your life vest on a jagged bit of its damaged body.

Surviving in the open sea

1 Whether you are in the water or have managed to get into your life raft:

a) Get clear and upwind of your helicopter as soon as possible (to avoid any problems if it catches fire) but stay near it until it sinks (if it hasn't sunk already).

b) Get clear of fuel-covered water in case the fuel catches fire.

c) Try to find other survivors – maybe your co-pilot or passenger hasn't managed to get into the life raft.

Action-Seeker Tip

Always approach a panicky survivor who's in trouble in the water from behind. That way there is less danger that they will kick, scratch, or grab you. Swim to a point directly behind them and grasp their life vest's backstrap. Now swim with the sidestroke to drag them to your raft.

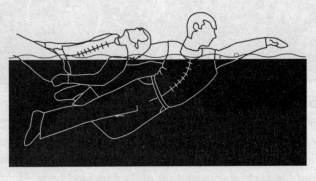

2 If you're in the water and not in your life raft:

a) Relax in the water. If you do there is very little danger that you will drown immediately. Your body's natural buoyancy (floatiness) will keep the top of your head above the sea water.

b) Float on your back if you can. It uses the least energy. Spread your arms and legs, and arch your back like this:

If you control your breathing, your face will always be out of the water. Believe it or not you can even take little naps in this position. Your head will be partly under the water, but your face will be above it.

3 Once you're in your life raft:

a) Throw out your sea anchor so you stay close to your ditched helicopter. This will make it easier for searchers to find you if you have signalled your location.

WARNING

With no sea anchor, your raft can drift more than 160 km a day!

Action-Seeker Tip

Wrap a cloth around your sea anchor's rope to stop it rubbing against your raft.

b) Check yourself and the other survivors for injuries. If you find any, use your first-aid kit immediately.

c) Find your emergency radio and get it working.

d) Tie material to an oar and raise it as high as possible to attract attention.

e) When you see a ship or aircraft, send up a flare.

f) Weigh up your situation and make a survival plan.

HAVE YOU BEEN PAYING ATTENTION?

1 Before ditching you must put on ...

a) some really nice aftershave.

b) a Michael Jackson CD.

c) a life vest.

2 As your helicopter sinks you will ...

a) be chatted up by some mermaids.

b) experience the 'cold-water-reflex'.

c) suddenly remember you can't swim.

3 To find the way to the surface if your life vest hasn't inflated properly you must ...

a) look at a map.

b) ask a passing fish.

c) blow a little air out of your mouth then follow the bubbles to the top.

4 Once your helicopter has filled with water you can ...

a) open the doors.

b) get out your sandwiches.

c) give up all hope.

5 As you rise to the surface, raise a hand above your head because ...

a) it looks really cool.

b) you must protect yourself from dangerous objects.

c) you desperately need to go to the toilet.

SURVIVING IF YOUR CHOPPER CATCHES FIRE IN MID-AIR

You're transporting some VIPs (very important people) to a top-level business meeting. There's not a cloud in the sky and you're chatting with your co-pilot about the joys of helicopter flying. You're flying straight and true at about 150 knots and the beautiful wooded hills below you are bathed in glorious winter sunshine. But then your co-pilot asks you if you can smell smoke. You sniff the air and, as you do, you notice blue wisps coming into the cabin from the direction of your chopper's engine housing. And the awful truth hits you. Your helicopter is on fire!

You are now faced with one of the most serious emergencies you'll have to deal with while you're flying. An engine fire! You have a huge amount of fuel in your tanks and at any moment the fire could reach them. Result: a huge explosion and a fireball that will severely and fatally barbecue both you and your passengers! Your number one priority is to get to the ground as quickly and safely as you can. Here's what you must do to survive this terrifying emergency:

1 Shut down your engine immediately. Your cabin is probably already filling up with poisonous fumes from the fire. So open your windows and doors to ventilate it.

2 Turn off your cabin heater to stop it sucking in smoke from your engine compartment.

3 Turn off your electrics – that's your battery and generator.

4 You must now do what is known as 'auto-rotating' your helicopter. In other words you've got to fly it to the ground without power. This is where your helicopter has the advantage over fixed-wing aeroplanes. As you go down, the rotor blades will continue to spin and prevent you from plummeting to Earth like a stone. It's like those winged seeds you see spinning down to earth from sycamore trees in the autumn.

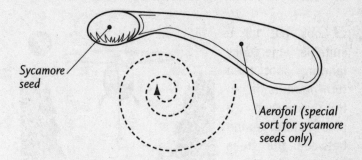

Sycamore seed

Aerofoil (special sort for sycamore seeds only)

So, in actual fact, what you're going to do is glide down to Earth. Auto-rotation is a good way to get to the ground when your helicopter engine catches fire because it's the fastest way to descend to Earth.

Auto-rotating your chopper

Auto-rotation is a tricky manoeuvre and requires lots of delicate touches on your controls and really precise timing. But it's possible. Helicopter pilots regularly practise auto-rotations so they can land safely if their engine fails when they're flying. Here's what you must do:

1 Lower your collective straightaway. This will keep your rotor blades spinning fast. If your rotor RPM drops too low during auto-rotation, your helicopter will instantly become an aeroplane without wings. Useless.

2 Use your cyclic to angle your rotor blades at a pitch that will keep you flying at about 60 knots.

3 Look out for a suitable emergency landing spot then turn towards it. In this situation, a piece of level ground between the trees would be ideal.

4 Turn into the wind. This will slow down your descent.

5 When you get to within 20–30 metres of the ground (about the height of a three-storey building), gently pull your cyclic back. This will tilt the nose of your chopper upwards.

6 When you're approximately five metres above the ground (about the height of three short circus acrobats), sharply pull on your collective to slow your rate of descent.

7 Push your cyclic forward to get your chopper level again. If you don't do this your skids may well dig into the ground when you make contact, causing your helicopter to flip over! However, if you do it too early you'll hit the ground at too great a speed ... which will also cause you problems!

8 You should now be landing your helicopter perfectly level and with little or no forward speed. Cushion the landing by raising your collective.

9 Phew, you're down! But you're not out of danger. Now that you've made contact with the ground you must immediately centre your cyclic and hold it completely still. Don't move your cyclic – this can cause the tail of your helicopter to hit the ground before the rest of the body and tail-first landings are bad news.

10 Now gently lower your collective.

11 Important! Before your passengers get out of the helicopter, warn them that the rotors will still be turning. In order to avoid losing their heads, they must duck under the main rotor and avoid walking back towards the tail rotor. Stay at your controls until the passengers are out from under the rotor so that you can prevent it from tipping down and hitting someone.

12 Get your co-pilot to escort any passengers away from the helicopter. They'll be really panicky and desperate to get away from the burning chopper. So even though you've warned them not to, they're still very likely to run in the direction of the tail rotor like a bunch of headless chickens (which they will soon become).

13 Well done, action-seeker. By keeping a *cool* head in a *hot* situation you've not only saved your own life, but the lives of your co-pilot and passengers too. (Pity about your chopper though.)

HAVE YOU BEEN PAYING ATTENTION?

1 Helicopter pilots regularly practise auto-rotations because ...
a) it saves them a fortune in fuel.
b) it enables them to land safely if their engine fails when they're flying.
c) they're all as thick as two planks.

2 During an auto-rotation, when you get 20–30 metres from the ground you must ...
a) gently pull your cyclic back.
b) leap out of your helicopter.
c) radio HQ and tell them to put the kettle on.

3 The best way to cushion your landing during auto-rotation is to ...

a) raise your collective.

b) raise your glasses.

c) raise your cyclic.

AVOIDING CRASHING YOUR CHOPPER DUE TO A WIRE STRIKE

The thing that kills more people in helicopter crashes than all other hazards put together is the accident known as the wire strike. This is when a helicopter is brought crashing to the ground after it flies into a cable or power line. Most modern countries are bristling with them and, when you're flying at 150 knots plus, they come up very fast and are very hard to spot. When you do, it's usually too late to do anything about it. A really big, strong cable can actually slice your helicopter in two! Here's how to avoid them:

1 Don't ever think you are too smart to fly into a wire or cable. Even when they know they're there, helicopter pilots sometimes fly into wires.

2 When you're fighting fires (see page 122), be especially careful to look out for cables because: **a)** they're often hidden by the smoke from the fire; and **b)** your heli-bucket and line can get snagged on them very easily!

3 If you're chasing criminals on the ground whilst flying your copper chopper (see page 114) be extra careful – you can be so caught up in the excitement of the chase that you fail to notice a power line and fly slap-bang into it.

4 Some power lines, poles and cables are brightly marked for safety. Look out for the special markings.

5 Power lines are also marked on maps, so check your maps before you fly and *while* you're flying.

6 If you're lucky, you may be flying a helicopter with power-line cutters on its nose. These are like a pair of giant secateurs which you operate from your cockpit. If you come up against a cable, use your cable snippers to cut it before it brings you down.

7 You may also have a 'cable proximity warning system' in your chopper. This uses magnetic field sensors, laser or radar to sense nearby wires, after which it sounds an alert as you're approaching them.

8 Be extra careful of smaller wires. Even an electric fence wire can bring your chopper down! If you spot horses, cows, pigs, etc there may be an electric fence nearby.

Heli-snippet

One helicopter pilot flying in Hong Kong crashed into a small kite made from paper and bamboo. The frame of the kite dented one of the chopper's blades and the nylon fishing line that it was held by wrapped around the control rods of the rotor assembly. The tension on the string made the chopper's controls stiff and difficult to work, but fortunately the pilot was able to land safely. If the line had been any stronger it would have certainly locked the controls and brought the helicopter down.

9 Always cross the wires at 45-degree angles and fly over the pylons, not the wires.

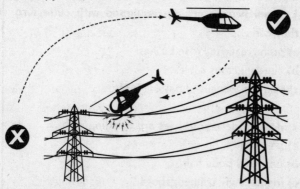

Your skids will get caught by the wire if you misjudge your height!

10 Ask your co-pilot and passengers to look out for wires and to tell you if they see them.

11 Watch out for wires against a blue sky or the sea. They're much harder to spot.

12 When you're landing somewhere you don't know well, do a slow, steep approach to give yourself time and space to avoid any wire that you haven't spotted earlier.

HAVE YOU BEEN PAYING ATTENTION?

1 Some helicopters are equipped with cutters so they can ...

a) prune really tall rose bushes.

b) cut dangerous cables.

c) trim the toenails of passing birds.

2 Most modern countries are bristling with ...

a) power lines.

b) unsightly body hair.

c) frighteningly tall hedgehogs.

SURVIVING A CRASH IN THE FROZEN NORTH

Imagine you've had to make an emergency landing in the icy frozen wastes of the North Pole or on the side of a snow-covered mountain in Alaska. Survival in the freezing cold is going to be really difficult, especially if your communications equipment is out of action and you're hundreds, perhaps even thousands, of kilometres from the nearest emergency services (not to mention a phone box which hasn't been vandalized by the local grizzly bears). Whether you come through this ordeal or not will all depend on your skill, determination and courage. And of course, how closely you pay attention to the following tips.

So, your helicopter's down, you aren't injured, you've got your emergency survival kit. But that's about it. The rest is up to you...

Keeping warm

1 Keep your head covered – perhaps with some fabric from the seats of your crashed chopper – but preferably not so much that you can't actually see where you're going.

Helicopter pilot (flightless)

Penguin (also flightless)

You can lose almost half your body heat from your head, neck, wrists and ankles if they aren't covered. There's hardly any fat on your head (unless of course, you happen to be a fathead) and cold soon affects the efficient working of your brain making you slow-witted and lacking in all common sense. (So, action-seeker, what's *your* excuse?)

Action-Seeker Tip

If you haven't got a sleeping bag, make one by folding any cloth material you find in your helicopter, then stuffing dry leaves, pine needles or moss between the layers. (But remember this is a sleeping bag, not a midnight snack.)

2 Make a shelter.

Action-Seeker Tip

Do *not* use your crashed helicopter for a shelter. Any heat you manage to create inside it will quickly be lost through your chopper's metal fuselage.

If you've crashed on a mountainside and there are forests around, you'll be able to build a shelter from tree branches and still have lots of wood available to make a fire. If you've crashed in the Arctic wastes where trees don't grow, you'll have to build a shelter from ice or snow. Snow and ice shelters include things like igloos and snow holes (these are the easiest to make if the snow's deep enough). For this you'll need tools like ice axes, saws, sharp knives (bulldozers, scaffolding and burly labourers).

Friend

Home

Dinner

3 Make a fire. Fire can save your life. You can cook food on it, get warmed by it and use it to melt snow or ice for water. You start a fire with tinder (dried moss, grass and twigs) and then put sticks and logs on the tinder. There are all sorts of styles in which you can construct your fire. For instance:

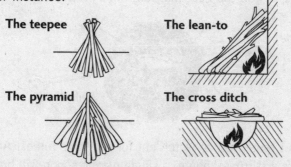

The teepee

The lean-to

The pyramid

The cross ditch

(and the much sought after, neo-Georgian villa).

Get a battery from your torch or electric tooth brush. Attach a wire to each terminal then touch the ends of the bare wires together. Position the battery so that the resultant sparks fall on to the tinder and ignite it.

Building a fire without wood

If you come down on the frozen pack ice of the Arctic, you won't have any wood for your fire. So you'll have to use a bit of ingenuity. However, if you can't find any of that, you could always use some of the fuel or oil from your crashed helicopter. Just drain a bit out of the tank when you need it. If you've not got anything to catch it in, don't worry. When it hits the ice it will congeal (go all lumpy) so just scoop dollops up as you need it. Keep your gloves on to do this as fuel can cause frostbite when it's really cold.

Here are some more things that burn really well and may give you the heat that may save your life:

Helmet   Tyre   Fantastic plastic

But remember to watch out for the toxic fumes! And here's a stirring thought: a single plastic spoon will burn for a whole ten minutes!

Getting rescued

At some point you'll no doubt get fed up with sitting around waiting to be rescued and, having noticed that your huge, regulatory, helicoper-pilot-stranded-in-the-wilderness-for-absolutely-yonks beard is now dangling several centimetres below your waist you'll no doubt want to set off in search of a decent hairdressing salon. This is not recommended. You should always stay at your crash site, as rescuers will find that first.

However, if you're desperate to go, always remember to leave clues showing which way you're going (e.g. make arrows out of sticks or stones showing the direction travelled).

Here are some tips to help you survive your trip:

1 Don't forget to take your EPIRB with you. It contains two radio transmitters and one GPS (Global Positioning System) receiver (but disappointingly, no MTV channel). While you're shivering in the snow, a mere 38,000 km above you a satellite notices that your EPIRB is transmitting a distress signal. Embedded in that signal is your own exclusive and totally unique serial number which gives your personal details, e.g. name, address, fave colour ... you get the idea. However that's not all! Thanks to the GPS receiver, the miraculous satellite is able to clock your exact precise position on the globe, e.g. three short steps to the left of that hungry polar bear!

2 Use rivers to find your way. If you follow them they may well lead to settlements where you'll meet people who'll help you out (if they don't have you for Sunday lunch).

3 Don't travel during blizzards. You may end up walking in circles for days on end.

4 Take care when crossing thin ice. Spread your weight by lying flat and crawling across it – but don't be tempted to stick your tongue on it as you wriggle your way across. It might instantly freeze to the ice leaving you stuck for the rest of your life (which will be quite short).

5 You'll find it impossible to walk through really deep snow. So, in order to spread your weight and not sink into the drifts, make yourself a pair of snowshoes (but not out of snow). The best materials are willow bark, strips of cloth or leather.

6 Make camp early so that you have plenty of time to build your shelter, make your fire, cook your meal (brush your teeth, comb your hair and say your prayers).

Action-Seeker Tip

You can have all the snazziest survival gear going but if you aren't really determined to survive you won't. You've got to have lots of will power.

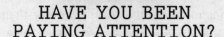

HAVE YOU BEEN PAYING ATTENTION?

1 If you've crashed on a mountainside and there are forests around about you'll be able to build a shelter from ...

a) lego bricks.

b) tree branches.

c) frozen spit.

2 You must always take extra care when crossing very thin ...

a) ice.

b) icing.

c) supermodels.

3 Don't travel during blizzards or you may end up walking in ...

a) circles.

b) triangles.

c) some polar bear poo.

FLYING YOUR CHOPPER IN REALLY BAD WEATHER

There is far more weather up in the sky than there is down on the ground. Some of it's quite nice but tons more is extremely nasty, and while you're flying it will frequently be doing its best to cause big, serious, gut-wrenching, bone-shaking, knee-knocking problems for you and your helicopter. Most sensible and experienced helicopter pilots avoid flying in really bad weather conditions but, being an action-seeker, at some time or other you will no doubt end up flying in snowy or stormy conditions. So here are lots of tips that will save your bacon (but only if you happen to be transporting some dead pigs).

Action-Seeker Tip

Keep a 'cloth' (sophisticated high-tech helicopter equipment used for wiping things) handy. Don't be caught out by your cockpit windscreen suddenly misting up in bad weather. Misting can be made even worse if you've got warm people in damp clothing on board, like a bunch of celebrities you've just rescued from kidnappers who've been holding them prisoner in a sauna. And even worse for steaming up cockpits are wet dogs – you may have these on board if you've flown them to a search and rescue operation. Your windscreen cloth may also come in useful for drying these wet dogs.

Dealing with thunderstorms

You've set off on a hot, sticky summer's afternoon. There's been a heatwave for weeks, but now, as you head for your destination, you spot massive purplish-black clouds billowing up on the horizon and hear distant rumbles. Soon the light changes to an eerie yellow colour and huge drops of rain begin to splatter against your windscreen. The wind suddenly increases dramatically, violently buffeting your chopper, making it feel no more stable than an airborne leaf! All at once a fork of lightning flashes across the horizon. It's closely followed by a deafening crack. Before you know it you're flying through the middle of a huge thunderstorm. Your helicopter is pushed this way and that and giant hailstones the size of golf balls begin bouncing off your fuselage. You pray that they won't damage your rotors. If they do you'll be in big trouble! But what should you do?

1 If you can, do a 180-degree turn and fly away from a storm.

2 If you can't avoid it, slow down your speed to whatever your helicopter's handbook recommends for these conditions. (However, it's not a good idea to actually try and read the handbook whilst undergoing this somewhat challenging experience.) Try and keep to a straight and level course that will get you through the storm as quickly as possible.

Action-Seeker Tip

Never get closer than eight km to a storm cloud that's got overhanging edges and looks like this:

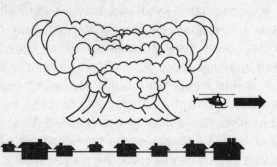

If you do, you'll probably get hammered by the mother of all hailstorms. Hail is one of the worst things about thunderstorm flying. Passing through it is like constantly being machine-gunned. Even as far away as 32 km from a really strong thunderstorm, you can be battered by hail and violent turbulence.

Some shocking facts about lightning

As well as doing really serious damage to your helicopter's body, lightning can also mess up its electrical systems including really crucial stuff like the instruments and the radar system. It can also do serious damage to you and your crew. Included in its unpleasant effects on humans are blindness (caused by the flash) electrical shocks, burns and deafness (from the shock waves).

The good news: Lightning strikes on helicopters are rare.

Flying in cold weather

1 Check your helicopter before you take off. If there are any bits of snow, ice or frost stuck to it, remove them before you take off. Even a teensy-weensy bit of ice on your rotor blades can upset the balance of your aircraft and have your whole chopper wobbling and vibrating like a jelly (after you've taken off, of course). And this, naturally, will lead to you losing control and plummeting to Earth.

One of the best ways to protect your helicopter and have it frost- and snow-free for a flight is to put it in the aircraft storage building known as a hangar.

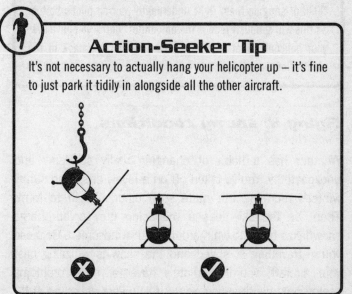

Action-Seeker Tip

It's not necessary to actually hang your helicopter up – it's fine to just park it tidily in alongside all the other aircraft.

2 Avoid cold wet bits. Try not to get wet before flying your helicopter, especially on really cold days. Your body, especially your sticky-out bits like feet and hands, can become extremely cold indeed when you fly up high in the air. Extreme cold can also affect your ability to think quickly and intelligently and may affect your ability to fly your helicopter and make a safe landing next to a five-star hotel that claims to have real log fires.

Action-Seeker Tip

Even if your hands are colder than a polar bear's fridge, do not be tempted to take them off your controls and blow on them, rub them or snuggle them right underneath your co-pilot's bottom as this will seriously reduce the amount of control you have over your helicopter (not to mention earning you a smack in the mouth from your co-pilot).

Flying in snowy conditions

Weather has a habit of changing really suddenly and unexpectedly. You've taken off on a lovely crisp and sunny winter's morning, but quite soon clouds begin to form. Then, as the sky goes a menacing grey colour, large snowflakes begin to whirl around your windscreen. Because you're travelling at speed and the snow is whizzing past your aircraft, you immediately have far more problems seeing properly than you would if you were standing still.

Now the snowstorm becomes a blizzard and you're soon struggling to make out where the land finishes and the sky begins. Soon you're flying in what's known as 'whiteout' conditions and your visibility has become absolute *zero*! In other words you might as well be flying with your eyes closed! This is not good news. You cannot distinguish up from down, right from left and back from front. It's almost like you're floating inside a pure white football!

If you do become disorientated like this, you will most certainly do the wrong things with your controls. This will make your helicopter behave quite crazily, which of course causes you to do even more wrong things with your controls. This is what is known as a vicious circle. The next thing you know you'll probably be involved in a high velocity impact and you will hit something large and solid at high speed (e.g. a mountain).

Action-Seeker Tip

If: **a)** you suddenly find all your money falling out of your pockets and your tie in your mouth; and **b)** you notice a herd of cows floating above you with their legs sticking up in the air ... you've probably begun flying upside down.

Ways to avoid a high-velocity impact in a snowstorm

1 Stay at home. Small plastic helicopters are on sale at most good toy shops and it really is tons of fun to run around your living room holding them above your head and making realistic rotor noises.

2 Use your intelligence, willpower and gumption (available in five and ten litre tins at most helicopter supplies outlets). When flying make sure that you're always well ahead of your helicopter.

This doesn't mean running in front of it while your co-pilot does the flying, nor does it mean sitting on the nose. It means think well ahead of yourself.

You'll probably be flying at over 150 knots so you need to rapidly anticipate problems up ahead, then take action to avoid dangerous areas where the visibility is obscured.

3 Before you set off, plan an escape route. Make note of visual references that you may be able to see, even in snow – distinguishing features like rocks, houses, trees or the black noses of passing polar bears (although the more mischievous ones may well put their paws over their noses to confuse you).

4 When it does start to snow, adjust your flight plans to take account of the conditions and safely land your helicopter as soon as you can.

5 In a serious snowstorm, look for those references you checked out earlier, then take that all-important escape route.

Flying in turbulence

Turbulence is another name for air that is moving roughly and unpredictably, often at great speed. If you've ever flown on an aeroplane you may have heard the warm, reassuring voice of the air steward announce that your aircraft is 'about to experience a little turbulence' after which you feel the craft begin to bump around quite alarmingly (and then its wings drop off). The main cause of turbulence is wind, especially wind moving around things like high buildings and trees in leaf.

Helicopters don't suffer as much from turbulence as some small fixed-wing aircraft because their flexible rotor blades absorb the movement rather than transferring it to the main body of the aircraft. However, when you attempt to land or take off in really high winds you've got big problems. When your rotors are only rotating quite slowly they will be drooping (rather pathetically) and the strong winds will cause them to flap about and clobber bits of your fuselage or even bash your tail rotor.

If you do have to take off on a windy day, look at the socks. That's the windsocks, not your own. They'll tell you which direction the wind is blowing in and give you an indication of just how strong it is.

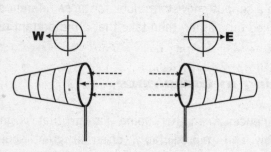

Action-Seeker Tip

As any experienced helicopter pilot will tell you, trying to hover in really windy conditions is a very difficult task (so avoid eating baked beans, pasta and cucumber sandwiches before takeoff).

HAVE YOU BEEN PAYING ATTENTION?

1 To protect your helicopter from frost, store it in ...
a) a fridge.
b) your rucksack.
c) a hangar.

2 If your cockpit windscreen mists up, wipe it with a ...
a) wet dog.
b) hot dog.
c) cloth.

3 As well as doing really serious damage to your helicopter's body, lightning can also ...
a) shrink the entire aircraft to the size of a baby sparrow.
b) mess up its electrical systems.
c) make your eyeballs fall out and bounce round the cockpit like ping-pong balls.

AVOIDING A BASHING BY BIRDS

Ever since humans began getting ideas above their stations and taking to the air, aircraft such as helicopters have become a real nuisance to birds, often forcing them to make inconvenient route changes and sometimes even to crash quite painfully. In the old days, when aircraft were slower, the birds could nip out of their way, but now that helicopters and many other winged aircraft are travelling faster, they get clobbered much more frequently.

Reassuring fact one: Most birds will do their best to get out of the way of your chopper.

Worrying fact one: For some reason best known to themselves, the large but pea-brained game birds known as pheasants are fond of screeching up out of the undergrowth and actually launching ferocious attacks on helicopters.

Even though most birds are tiny compared to a helicopter ...

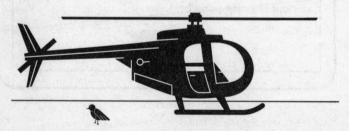

... running into one can cause serious damage to your chopper. A bump with a bird can lead to bent or broken rotor blades blocked engine air intakes and a smashed windshield.

Reassuring fact two: Only one in a hundred bird strikes occur above 900 metres. Why? Because most birds fly below that level (they've no head for heights).

Worrying fact two: Most bird strikes occur on landing and takeoff.

If you want to prevent having your flight disrupted by birds you must:

1 Check your chopper before takeoff. Birds can build their nests really quickly and you might find that while your chopper has been parked a pair of sparrows have built a cosy little home for eight in your air inlet (or flying helmet). This sort of thing could interfere with your instruments or even cause a fire once you're in mid-air. Watch out for tell-tale signs of nest-building and mating such as heaps of twigs, grass and leaves (or rows of baby-bird nappies dangling from your rotor blades), then carefully remove the hazard (after having explained to the birds the reasons for your actions in a caring and sensitive manner).

2 Avoid flying along rivers or shorelines, especially at low altitude. Not having yet perfected a suitably small atlas, or a global positioning system, birds (as well as helicopter pilots) use these natural features to find their way.

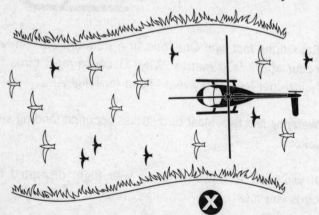

3 Avoid big wet places like lakes and estuaries where large numbers of gulls, waders and waterfowl are in the habit of going for regular evening or early morning spins round the block.

4 Stay well clear of offshore islands, headlands, cliffs, inland waters and shallow estuaries, so as not to disturb nesting colonies.

⚠ WARNING

Don't think that just because you're flying at night you're safe from bird strikes – you're not! As well as flying during the daytime some birds are in the habit of flitting about in the dark – frequently without lights! And bats are just as irresponsibly dangerous.

Three times of the year to be especially careful of birds:
a) Autumn – when many British birds are gathering in huge flocks and setting off on their winter hols to places like Africa and South America.
b) Spring – when they're all coming back again (loaded down with duty free birdseed).
c) July and August – when there are lots of young and inexperienced learner birds taking flying lessons and getting to grips with manoeuvres that will enable them to survive, e.g. the three-point tern.

HAVE YOU BEEN PAYING ATTENTION?

1 Birds' eyesight is ...

a) ten times sharper than that of humans.

b) so powerful they can see through walls.

c) much improved when they eat heaps of carrots.

2 To cut down the possibility of being hit by birds you must ...

a) cover your helicopter in light-brown feathers.

b) avoid flying over estuaries.

c) make tweeting noises as you fly.

3 Most bird strikes occur ...

a) when battery chickens want better pay and conditions.

b) when it's a hen night down the bowling alley.

c) on landing and takeoff.

How to ...
be a heli-hero

IDENTIFYING HELICOPTERS AND THE JOBS THEY DO

Helicopter gunships
Operates in war zones.

Transport helicopters
Carries large numbers of people and heavy equipment.

Gyroplane
Used for leisure flights and pilot training.

Aircrane helitanker
Used for firefighting. Drops fire retardant foam and water onto large blazes.

Air-ambulance
Gets seriously ill and injured people to hospital as quickly as possible.

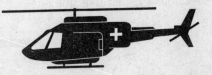

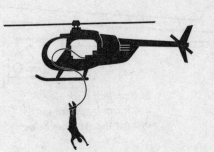

Leisure chopper
Carries skiers and bungee jumpers.

Tourist chopper
For sightseeing trips.

BEING A CHOPPER COPPER

One of the most exciting, action-packed and useful jobs you can do as a helicopter pilot is to work with a Police Air Support Unit. This all-action occupation involves whizzing around in a copper chopper, giving back up to your police colleagues down on the ground as they chase stolen cars, bring bad guys to justice, ferret out fugitives (and face down fugitive ferrets). You'll be flying a state-of-the-art, specialized machine, bristling with the latest technology, just like this one:

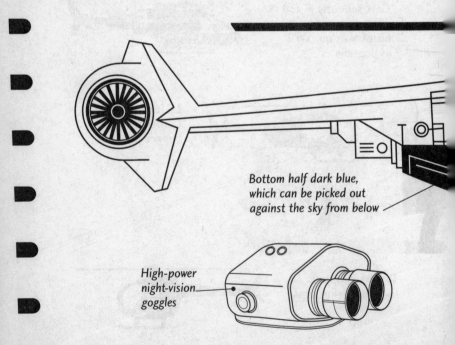

Bottom half dark blue, which can be picked out against the sky from below

High-power night-vision goggles

And when it comes to operating efficiency there'll be nothing to touch you; when you're working with all the stops pulled out, you and your chopper will be doing as much work as 15 police cars down on the ground. And, unlike those earthbound cop cars, you won't be slowed down by traffic jams or one-way systems. Flying at speeds of up to 240 km/h (yes, that's almost four kilometres every minute!) you'll be able to whizz to incidents in double-quick time. And that really is the trick to nailing baddies.

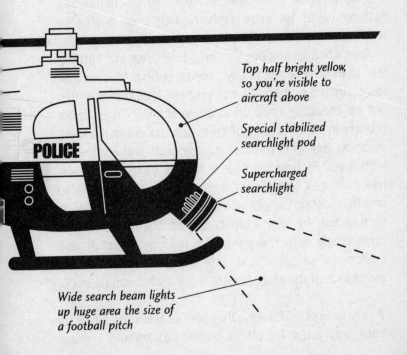

Top half bright yellow, so you're visible to aircraft above

Special stabilized searchlight pod

Supercharged searchlight

POLICE

Wide search beam lights up huge area the size of a football pitch

115

But while you're thwarting thieves you must always be aware that this flying law-enforcement miracle you're piloting hasn't come cheap. It will have cost around about three million pounds and for every hour you're in the air it costs £800! So your responsibilities are enormous. At all times you must fly safely and considerately, avoiding prangs with carelessly parked hot-air balloons, plummeting meteorites and flocks of short-sighted racing pigeons. And of course whenever you land, you must always make a careful note of the precise location where you left your super-chopper as nothing could be more embarrassing than having to report back to HQ and say you accidentally 'lost it'.

As a chopper copper you and your crew are nothing less than an 'eye in the sky', seeing behind fences, over walls, around corners. One of your really essential duties will be providing back up at crime scenes. Like a bank robbery in which a gang of criminals has entered a bank in broad daylight, threatening the staff and customers with guns. Picture the scene. As one of the customers has managed to slip out and raise the alarm (not to mention obtain a generous bank loan), the bank is surrounded by police officers and the incident has turned ugly with the gangsters holding the staff and customers hostage and threatening to shoot them. Your assistance at the siege is vital. Here's what you must do:

1 Fly in special forces. Once you've received a call for back up, you'll fly off to collect: a) trained hostage situation negotiators who will talk to the robbers in an attempt to end the siege peacefully; **b)** police dog handlers and their dogs who will bark menacingly throughout the siege (the dogs, not the handlers); and **c)** trained police marksmen in case shooting breaks out.

2 Get to the incident. You must now fly to the scene of the crime as quickly and safely as possible.

3 Use your navigation aids. You may well be unfamiliar with the area over which you're flying. But don't worry. You won't be troubled by the inconvenience of having to put down every few seconds and ask for directions. Your helicopter is equipped with a space-age navigation system. By receiving information beamed down from a satellite orbiting high above the earth this amazing piece of kit instantly informs you as to exactly which bit of the world you're in.

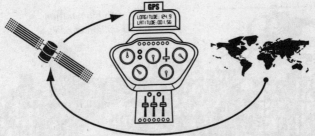

In fact, these state-of-the-art gadgets can actually pick out individual addresses in areas in which there are thousands and thousands of houses – even if some of them have been cunningly disguised to look just like all the others! And naturally, just in case all that high-tech stuff ever fails, your cockpit is also fully equipped with good old-fashioned paper maps and atlases.

4 Take stock of the situation. Once you reach the incident, hover at a safe distance above the siege, taking care not to slice off local residents' chimney pots and TV aerials or wake sleeping babies. You'll be slightly quieter than some other helicopters because you don't have a conventional tail rotor. This reduces the noise of your machine by 50 per cent (which of course makes sneaking up on stone-deaf car thieves a doddle).

5 Light up the scene. If the siege has lasted so long that darkness has now fallen, you must now illuminate the scene below with the amazing '30-million-candle' search-aid which is mounted beneath the front of your helicopter.

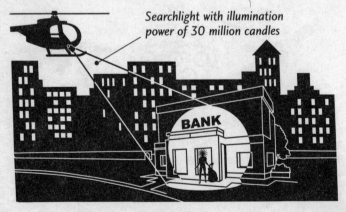

Searchlight with illumination power of 30 million candles

6 Deliver the specialists. Having illuminated the area you should be able to identify a suitable landing spot. Put down as quickly as you can. Once the marksmen, dogs and negotiators are safely out you can take off again.

7 Call for order. Positioned underneath your helicopter are two sets of loud-hailers. They've got an output of 700 watts so when they're used at full volume they're about ten times louder than the average home hi-fi system. If a huge crowd has now gathered to watch the action, order them to stay well away from the danger area. Also instruct nearby residents to evacuate their homes.

8 Film the action. Mounted in a pod on the nose of your chopper is a super-duper TV camera linked to a screen in your cockpit that can zoom in on a person or object and magnify them or it 54 times. And if you think that's amazing, it's said that boffins in the USA have now developed a long-range camera that will enable a helicopter pilot to read a car number plate from *11 km* away (but only if they're wearing their reading glasses).

9 Relay the information. Your camera system is linked to a video machine which not only records everything you're filming but sends live pictures back to HQ via what is known as a 'microwave downlink'. So as you hover it's essential that you video all of the action, zooming in on the faces of the gang the moment you get a chance so that your colleagues can use their huge databank to identify the baddies.

10 Give chase. Suddenly two of the robbers burst out of the bank using a hysterically screaming and sobbing hostage as a human shield (he's a real wimp, that bank manager). They hijack a high-powered sports car parked in the next street and roar off, scattering police officers and onlookers as they go. You follow, easily keeping pace with them, keeping your search beam on their speeding vehicle and constantly relaying details of their exact position to your colleagues in patrol cars down on the ground.

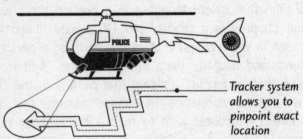

Tracker system allows you to pinpoint exact location

11 Corner the criminals. Unable to evade the ever-present beam of your searchlight, the baddies have now panicked. They've abandoned both their car and their hostage and run off into a dense wood, hoping to melt away under cover of the pitch-black night. But they've reckoned without you, your night-vision goggles and your FLIR! Mounted in a pod on the nose of your chopper – yes, another pod – is what is known as a Forward

Looking InfraRed (or FLIR). This is a camera-based thermal-imaging device which pinpoints warm objects such as people, animals, cars and power lines, then shows them up on a screen in your chopper.

12 Make the arrest. As your FLIR system enables body heat to be detected from hundreds of metres away, you have no problem locating the robbers as they crouch in the thick undergrowth. You radio instructions to your colleagues on the ground who release their tracker dogs. The dogs soon nose out the baddies and you, action-seeker, clock up another heroic victory.

Heli-snippet

Two men fell from a bridge into the freezing cold River Tyne in Newcastle. No one could get them out so after 20 minutes the police helicopter was sent for. When it arrived they were in the middle of the river and were both exhausted. One was clutching a life belt and the other was being swept away by the powerful current. The police helicopter pilot immediately hovered his chopper over the men and then cleverly used the downdraught from his rotor blades to blow them to the river bank. If the men had been in the water much longer they undoubtedly would have drowned!

HAVE YOU BEEN PAYING ATTENTION?

1 You use your loud-hailer to ...
a) warn the public of danger.
b) tell criminals to give themselves up.
c) lead mass police singsongs.

2 Your FLIR can pinpoint criminals in the dark by ...
a) sniffing out their sweaty armpits.
b) detecting their body heat.
c) videotaping what they're thinking.

USING YOUR HELICOPTER TO PUT OUT A HUGE FOREST FIRE

The wild hills of Southern California are covered with massive forests and every year at the end of the long hot summer these woods get tinder dry. All it needs is a carelessly dropped cigarette, an abandoned campfire, a fallen power line, (or a clumsy fire-eater) to create a blaze. Sometimes fires even start from spontaneous combustion caused by the sun's intense heat. Driven on by 110-km/h winds that come sweeping up from the south, a huge forest fire is soon raging through the hills. In no time at all, thousands of acres of trees and bushes are blazing and hundreds of homes are threatened by the raging inferno. Roads become jammed with emergency vehicles that are coming to the rescue and the cars of panic-stricken people who are trying to escape the blaze. Fire engines on their way to fight the fires are caught up in these jams and as a result many people are left to defend their houses on their own. Some of these houses are so isolated that, even without any chaos on the roads, it's almost impossible for fire engines to reach them.

As the firestorm rages it quickly becomes apparent that some families and some of the firefighters who've managed to get through are now trapped by the flames and soon their situation is beginning to appear desperate. Huge clouds of blue-black smoke cause their eyes to stream with tears and their throats feel like they're being rubbed red-raw with sandpaper. The inferno is now so intense that just a short way away from them trees are actually *exploding* from the heat as the sap and water inside them is *instantly* brought to boiling point by the massive temperatures. Terrified people look on. It really does look like the end is near for each and every one of them.

Suddenly, above the noise of the flames they hear the growl of rotors. The next moment there is huge roar and a deafening whooshing noise followed by angry sizzling and spluttering sounds as thousands of gallons of water cascade from your chopper onto the inferno below. The trapped people give a huge cheer. You and your miraculous air-crane helitanker have arrived just in time.

Your air-crane helitanker

Lucky owners of the helitanker should recognize their machine from this picture. It is a miraculous invention, nothing less than a giant flying fire engine! It's 26 metres long (that's longer than a juggernaut lorry) and attached to it is a huge tank, big enough to carry 11,000 litres of water (or 11,000 litres of designer fragrance if you're rescuing top fashion models).

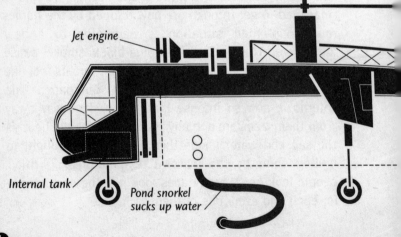

Jet engine

Internal tank

Pond snorkel
sucks up water

In addition to the water tank your helicopter has a 300-litre 'internal' tank. This carries special fire-retardant foam which you can inject into your main tank so that it mixes with the water in there. By some cunning means, known only to boffins with big hair and sticky-out teeth, the foam breaks the water's surface tension. That helps the water stick to leaves and twigs more easily so when the fire reaches them they're coated with a flame resistant barrier (clever, or what?).

And, of course, you don't just have to rely on the water to quell the inferno that's raging below you. Conveniently situated in your nose you've got a front-mounted foam cannon which can shoot a huge torrent of that fire-retardant foam up to a distance of nearly 45 metres – and the foam cannon mounted in the helicopter's nose is quite effective too.

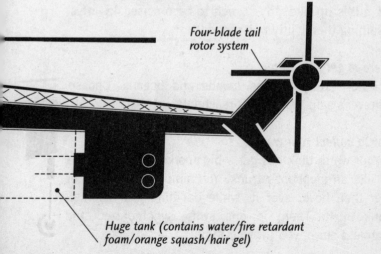

Four-blade tail
rotor system

Huge tank (contains water/fire retardant
foam/orange squash/hair gel)

Getting your water supply

Even 11,000 litres of water doesn't go far when you're trying to put out a fire that covers an area the size of Shropshire. But there's no need to panic, your helitanker is capable of delivering 136,000 litres of water every single hour that you're in action. Naturally, that means refilling your giant water tank over and over again, but your super-chopper is definitely up to the job. It can lift over 12 tons of water in one go! And when you've dropped your first massive load of water onto the fire you simply fly to the nearest water supply and fill up again.

Even if the nearest water's a little way off, it isn't a problem! Your giant helicopter can fly at around 160 km/h so it can get to water sources and back to the fire-ravaged area in the blink of several, smoke-filled eyes. And it fills up in a jiffy ... well to be precise, 45 jiffys (assuming that 1 jiffy = 1 second).

Where to get your water
Look for streams, lakes, ponds and oceans. Choose whatever's safe, handy and reachable.

How to collect your water
a) Your water tank has got a big snorkel nozzle on it, a bit like an elephant's trunk. You simply find a lake or river then hover over it, while dangling your snorkel-trunk in it. Then, in one swift, synchronized and seamless slurp, you fill your tank.

b) If you don't want to hang around sucking up your water you can also sort of shovel it up from the sea or a lake using the ram scoop hydrofoil. And it will only take around 45 seconds to refill your tank this way too.

WARNING

Take great care when you're scooping. Some very large fire-fighting aircraft have been known to scoop up swimmers in their desperate rush to collect water.

c) Sometimes you may be supplied with water from a dip tank hauled behind a truck that's parked a safe distance away from the fire.

If you don't think you're ready for a huge helitanker you might like to try firefighting with something a bit smaller (e.g. a water pistol). Smaller firefighting helicopters use state-of-the-art water-buckets which you simply lift with the help of a hook on the end of a cable that trails from your helicopter (a bit like hook-a-duck but slightly more challenging). They have a fast-fill facility and you can control the rate at which the water flows out of the bucket. And if you don't want to drop it all in one go, its multi-dump valve will allow you to target several different areas.

Of course, hovering over blazing infernos and quelling raging forest fires is by no means a piece of cake. The whole operation is fraught with danger and requires the greatest levels of skill, courage, concentration and planning.

Mission hazards

1 Cables and wires. You already know about these from page 85.

2 Trees. If you're using a dump bucket they can get tangled up with your cable and bring you crashing to the ground, probably just where the fire's at its worst. Stay well above them.

3 Flames. These great tongues of fire rise more than 60 metres into the air and leap huge gaps between trees. You've got litres and litres of high octane aviation fuel on board. Intense heat or one careless swoop that brings you just too near the fire could turn your helicopter into a fireball in an instant! Stay high enough to avoid them.

4 Large mountains. Don't forget, you're often putting out fires in steep mountainous areas so you've got very little room for manoeuvring if things go wrong. Just clip a tree top or rock with a rotor blade and you're in big trouble. You'll need eyes in the back of your head on this mission!

5 Smoke. It's almost always thickest where you want to dump your water. In other words, the spot where the fire's at its worst.

How to ... be a heli-hero

Action-Seeker Tip

If you're brave and skilful enough to keep your chopper in an extended hover just above the fire you can use your rotor downwash to blow smoke away. This means that people who are trying to fight the flames or escape from them will have more chance of seeing what they're doing and it will also keep down the risk of them choking to death on the thick poisonous smoke.

WARNING

If you can't see through the smoke, don't fly into it. There's no telling what it might be hiding: other helicopters, small spotter planes, power lines, trees (the Empire State Building, the open jaws of a Tyrannosaurus Rex).

6 Other aircraft. There may be several other water-dumping helicopters in the area as well as the light spotter helicopters which are coordinating the mission. With lots of aircraft aloft, and the smoke and confusion of the fire, the risk of your having a mid-air collision is high! Constant and precise radio communication with everyone else involved is essential.

7 Weather changes. The weather affects the fire and the fire affects the weather resulting in unpredictable air currents and general turbulence. While you're fighting the fire you'll be doing long periods of hovering at below 150 metres. That's when you may find things like sudden updraughts of air having a really bad effect on your ability to control your helicopter. Be ready for them so they don't catch you by surprise.

8 Sudden changes in weight. When you've dropped your water, or part of it, the sudden change in the weight of your load will instantly have a drastic effect on the way your helicopter handles. Be prepared for this!

9 Clobbering the people you're supposed to be helping. While you're scooping or sucking up water from ponds or lakes, you may unintentionally gather up rocks or chunks of wood. When you let your load go, these dangerous objects will go with it and possibly land on the people below you. Try to avoid collecting water from places where you might accidentally pick up this sort of thing.

Heli-snippet

One group of firefighting helicopters with water-buckets were called to put out a fire in a skyscraper in Hong Kong. The fire engines on the ground were having difficulty reaching the blaze due to narrow streets and traffic congestion. The most convenient water supply for the choppers to fill up their buckets were some enormous tanks which were quite near by. So they filled their buckets and flew to the fire. As they emptied their buckets and the water cascaded onto the inferno below, people noticed that in addition to the water, also falling from the sky, were thousands of ... *fish*! The water tanks had belonged to the local fish farm!

HAVE YOU BEEN PAYING ATTENTION?

1 The best places to get water from are ...
a) ponds and lakes.
b) paddling pools full of happy toddlers.
c) streams and rivers.

2 To put out a fire, your helitanker sprays it with a mixture of water and ...
a) hair gel.
b) special fire-retardant foam.
c) special fire-retardant fun-foam.

CARRYING OUT A HELICOPTER RESCUE AT SEA

You're the pilot captain of a SAR (Search and Rescue) helicopter. Your crew consists of you, your co-pilot, your winch operator and your winchman (also known as 'the-dope-on-the-rope'), who may also act as a rescue swimmer. You're based on a wild and stormy coastline and can be called out at any moment for all sorts of emergencies, including rescuing people stuck on cliffs, small children washed out to sea on life rafts, ditched aircraft and boats in all kinds of trouble.

You're sitting in your base on a dark and stormy winter's afternoon when the coastguard sounds the alarm hooter. You rush to the phone and are briefed on the situation. A fishing boat is in trouble about 95 km down the coast. It's taking in water and it's being driven towards huge rocks by mountainous seas. There are four people on board and another has been washed overboard. It's down to you whether these people survive or perish. Time is of the essence. Here's what you must do:

1 Get 'suited and booted'. In other words put on your rubber immersion suit, your life vest and 'bone-dome', then make your way to your chopper as fast as you can.

2 Complete the pre-flight safety checks, then take off. The ground crew will have done some of these while you were getting kitted up.

3 As you fly to the scene, the coastguard radios you more details about the situation. Your co-pilot notes these while you're busy keeping your chopper in the air as you're buffeted by gale-force winds and lashed by torrential rain. You're used to this kind of thing though. Bad weather goes with emergencies at sea. You can cope with all sorts, including fog, snowstorms and ice on your rotor blades

4 You reach the scene and see that a fishing boat is being tossed about by huge waves that are bringing it closer and closer to jagged rocks under a towering cliff face. When it reaches those rocks it will be smashed to pieces. Your task is to get the crew off the boat before that happens.

5 Drop marine markers (flares) or electric sea-marker lights, so you know where the boat is. In these mountainous seas and the rapidly growing darkness you could easily lose its position again. And discuss the best course of action with your team.

Rescuing the man overboard

You decide that your first priority is the crew member in the sea.

1 In order to locate them, hover your chopper as low as you dare without endangering the lives of yourself and your crew. Your co-pilot will talk you into position, occasionally warning you to dodge one of the giant waves which would certainly smash you into the cliff face or the sea.

Action-Seeker Tip

Always hover into the wind. This will give you more stability and better control over your chopper.

2 Your team scans the giant waves and your winchman suddenly spots a tiny yellow dot but then it disappears again, swallowed by a wave the size of a house. It's the man overboard. Fortunately, he's wearing a bright yellow life vest (not to mention a rather repulsive acrylic cardigan).

3 Immediately select the 'overfly' mode on the control panel of your state-of-the-art SAR chopper.

Because it's so easy to lose a sighting in these conditions, this ingenious computer-generated device notes the position of the man overboard, automatically flies your chopper in a circuit, then puts it in auto-hover mode above the exact spot you saw the survivor ... all at the flick of a switch!

4 As you auto-hover, your winch operator will now use the joystick control lever in the back of your chopper to position the helicopter exactly above the drowning man. Once in position, the heroic winchman will now be lowered on the cable so that he can carry out his rescue swim.

5 Because of the winds, the winchman, or rescue swimmer, is swinging around like Tarzan on the end of the cable. Your winch operator now has to raise or lower him according to the sea conditions. When a swell comes up, they'll drop them into the water. Then, as the wave drops away they'll let out more cable as fast as possible so that the poor old rescue swimmer isn't suddenly yanked back up.

6 On reaching the drowning fisherman, your winchman fits him into a double strop. This is a type of harness with one strop that goes around his chest and under his arms and another to go under his knees. Your winchman hangs about 30 cm higher than the person he's rescuing with his legs around their arms so they can't accidentally raise them and slip out of the harness.

Heli-snippet

The double strop is needed to stop 'thermal shock' caused by the blood running to the legs. This can be fatal as was found in the 1979 Fastnet Race disaster when most of the survivors rescued died in the helicopter after some nine hours in the water.

7 The winchman will then make the thumb-up 'ready for hoist' signal to you and the winch operator, who hoists him up. He then finally helps the survivor into the helicopter. Phew!

Rescuing the rest of the crew

1 You take over the controls of your chopper again, as you're now going to rescue the people on the boat. First you lower your heli-basket. The winchman will go down in it to make sure the fishing crew know what to do.

2 Lowering the basket is a tricky and mega-dangerous operation because: **a)** the giant seas are rising and falling constantly and the distance between you and the boat deck decreases and increases dramatically every few moments; **b)** if you aren't careful, you could easily snag the heli-basket line on the equipment on the fishing boat's deck, bringing your aircraft crashing down or severely injuring your winchman; and **c)** as you hover, you could easily skewer your chopper on one of the boat's radio masts or crash into the wires that run between them.

3 If you haven't got radio contact with the people on the ship, lower a VHF radio on the end of a bright-orange line weighted down with bits of metal to stop it swinging about too much.

4 Helicopters create a massive amount of static electricity. It's really important for your winchman to make sure the crew don't touch him before he's touched their boat or the sea. Otherwise they'll receive a big electric shock! Let them know this.

5 As they're directly below your chopper, you won't be able to see the basket or the boat. Your winch operator will now be your eyes and ears. Speak to him through his microphone. He'll tell you how to move. He'll also tell you where your basket is.

An interesting point: it would be possible for you to leave your ultra-modern helicopter on auto-hover and, along with your co-pilot and winch operator, clamber into the heli-basket and go down to the fishing boat, leaving your chopper hovering above you all on its own! However, this isn't recommended!

6 You've been in the air for quite some time now and your fuel's running low! Your co-pilot will be calculating how much longer you can remain at the scene. Make sure he keeps you up to speed on this vital information.

7 Because of the noise of the wind and waves, and the roar of your helicopter, your winchman will use hand signals (see page 58) to communicate with your winch operator.

8 Once the basket is on the ship's deck, the winchman helps the fishermen into it, telling them to keep their arms and legs inside at all times and not to reach out and try to grab anything or try and help. They could get badly hurt.

9 The basket now arrives at your helicopter. Your winch operator, who's held in with a safety belt, will reach out and pull the basket into the chopper.

10 That's it! Well done, action-seeker – you've saved five lives! Now you must fly the soaked and exhausted fishermen to the local hospital as quickly as possible. But remember, you'll be very tired now so you must concentrate *extra* hard on flying safely!

HAVE YOU BEEN
PAYING ATTENTION?

1 When you get an SAR call out, you must put on ...

a) a rubber dinghy.

c) a rubber immersion suit.

d) a brave face.

2 When you spot the stricken boat drop ...

a) marker flares.

b) your trousers.

c) electric sea-marker.

3 One way of rescuing a group of people on a sinking boat is by lowering ...

a) a picnic basket.

b) a heli-basket.

c) their expectations.

Conclusion

Congratulations, action-seeker! You've done it! You've taken the first giant step towards finding out what it means to be an action-seeking helicopter pilot. Quite soon, after practice, you'll find that mastering the controls of your chopper becomes second nature, like riding your bike or operating your PC. And as you can carry out all those challenging and complex manoeuvres almost without thinking, you'll then be able to concentrate on all the really thrilling, glamorous and useful stuff. Stuff like: finding boy scouts lost on snow-covered mountain tops (just moments before severe frostbite causes their woggles to drop off); daring stunt-flying in blockbusting action movies; whizzing top movie stars, sports celebs and politicians to glamorous get-togethers at remote luxury castles and private island hideaways; transporting TV news cameramen to cover top sporting and news events; airlifting valuable racehorses from cliff ledges (where they've thrown themselves after coming last in the Grand National) ... the list is endless! And if that lot all becomes a bit tedious (ha ha) you can always become a crime-busting chopper copper or carry out peace-keeping duties by flying a miltary helicopter in one of the world's troublespots. And when you've achieved all that, there's always that non-stop hovering record to break, not to mention taking part in the heli-Olympics where chopper pilots compete in thrilling stuff like obstacle races and heli-aerobatics! So, auto-rotator, do it sooner rather than later ... go fly!

Glossary

There are lots of words you'll use as a helicopter pilot that are special to the thrilling world of choppers and aviation. Here are some of them:

aerofoil a curved surface designed to produce 'lift' when air is passed over it above sea level

altitude the height your helicopter is flying at

attitude the angle at which your helicopter flies in relation to the ground

angle of pitch the angle between your rotor blades and the plane of the main rotor hub

approach paths the flight routes you use to fly in to landing spots such as helipads and heliports

auto-rotation the technique by which you switch off your engine then use your helicopter's rotor blades to make a safe descent (or dry your hair when you've just come out of the shower)

cockpit the part of the helicopter which you and your passengers sit in and which contains all the main controls

cushion-of-ground air effect the effect by which your rotor wash hits the ground then sort of 'pings' back at your chopper to give you extra 'whumph' when you're taking off

clean air air which isn't affected by the cushion-of-air ground effect, i.e. mainly the sort that's up in the sky

cyclic pitch control the lever you use to change the pitch of your rotor blades individually

collective pitch control the lever you use to change the pitch of all your rotor blades equally and at the same time

effective translational lift (ETL) the additional lift you achieve because your rotor system becomes more efficient in certain circumstances – for instance when you're flying at speed

fixed-wing aircraft an aeroplane with wings that don't spin

FLIR (forward looking infrared) a heat-recognizing device which enables you to detect warm objects in the dark, e.g. escaped criminals, lost children, piping-hot steak-and-kidney puddings

fuselage the main body of your helicopter

GPS (global positioning system) a computer-aided device which enables you to discover your exact position anywhere in the world

helipad a spot specially designated and marked for landing helicopters on

heliport an airport specifically designed for helicopters to land at

heli-basket large basket-shaped container for rescuing groups of people from sinking ships or the rooftops of burning buildings

heli-bucket a large container for scooping up water to tip on fires

hover mode keeping your helicopter in a fixed position above a specific point on the ground

Jesus nut the nut that holds your rotor assembly together (and tells you to mend your ways)

rotor shaft the central metal rod to which your helicopter's rotor blades are attached

torque a force or combination of forces that cause the fuselage of a single rotor helicopter to rotate clockwise as its rotor turns counterclockwise

anti-torque pedals the pedals that control the tail rotor which is attached to most single main rotor helicopters in order to counteract the torque effect

NOTARS (no tail rotors) a helicopter where the tail rotor is replaced by a gas turbine thingymajig designed to counteract the torque effect

rescue strop a harness used in conjunction with a winch to lift people out of the sea or other perilous situations

rotor wash the powerful draught of air caused by the spinning of your helicopter's rotor blades

rotary-wing aircraft an aircraft that has a wing or wings which spin* rather than remaining stationary (*NB if this happens when you're flying a Boeing 747 or Harrier Jump Jet stop immediately – there is something seriously wrong with your aircraft)

RPM (revolutions per minute) the amount of times your rotor blades spin during one minute

SAR (search and rescue) the procedure in which specially trained teams set off to look for lost sailors, hikers, mountain climbers (or similar nincompoops) then rescue them from whatever sort of predicament they find themselves in

skids horizontal, metal landing bars attached to smaller types of helicopters

winch a powerful hoisting machine particularly used in helicopters designed for search and rescue operations

windsock a hollow cone of orange material used for indicating wind direction at heliports and airfields (also look rather pretty on breezy days)

wire snipper device attached to nose of your helicopter for cutting cables so they don't cause you to crash

wire strike what happens when your helicopter flies into a power line or cable of some sort